# Heaven's Register

## Reb Moshe

**First Edition Published May 2006**

**ISBN 0-9552969-0-0,**

**ISBN 978-0-9552969-0-1,**


Distributed and Published by
"Reb Moshe" Publishing
82 Coniston Road, Muswell Hill
London N10 2BN, United Kingdom
Tel 0794 1810216
International callers +44 794 1810216

We Dedicate This Book

"Heavens Register"

To Each and Everyone of You

To The Spiritually Enlightened and Blessed Generation

All Members of the Eternal Divine Heavens Register

# Contents

# Chapter 1

*"What we call life, is a wonderful journey - full of purpose.
When the mission is realized the person passes away.
This is the eternal law of nature".*

## Introduction and Meaning of Heaven's Register

Every single human being on planet earth is unique. No two people are the same nor can they be, nor will they ever be the same. This inherent unique gift of individuality of every single person is given to identify that each and every person has a specific mission, a goal in life that only that person can accomplish.

According to the teachings of the Talmud tractate Sotah 2a, every single soul is written into a Divine Heavenly Register of souls. The whole map of the journey of one's life is written into the heavenly register of records, known as the akashic records, with all the specific purposes and reasons one's soul has entered this physical world, the tests, the circumstances, the places where one will live, all the members of one's soulgroup one will meet and when, how one will earn a livelihood, and when and how one will meet one's true soulmate.

All the most vital and important destined meetings one's soul must experience at the exact and specific times during one's lifetime are written into the heavenly register.

The existence of these records in heavens register enables spiritually sensitive people, psychics and mediums, through the spiritual communication with their guardian angels, the ability to access these records to see the past, present and future, what needs to be done and corrected in one's life to find one's true destined purpose and pathway. This is the innate reason why many people seek spiritual help from mediums, psychics and palmists, as a confirmation that they are on the correct pathway, in accordance with the records in heavens register.

This book heaven's register will teach you how to use such feelings, how to allow yourself to be guided by your guardian angels such as how to use wisely the instantaneous magnetic attraction towards certain people at specific places at exact times and how to make such destined occurrences happen in one's life

Heaven's Register explains the basic spiritual principles to enable everyone to find one's true destiny in life. If one has been misled or strayed from one's pathway, then through the knowledge in this book one will be able to connect with one's guardian angels and find one's way back destined home, to the place of one's true destiny, living a purposeful, happy and enlivened life with one's true soulmate.

"What we call life, is a wonderful journey - full of purpose. When the mission is realized the person passes away. This is the eternal law of nature". Whomsoever we are and whatever religion, nationality or soulgroup we belong to, we are all spiritual souls within a physical body created by the same eternal Divine spirit of GOD, the creator of the whole universe. We are all born for this journey of life, and once our purpose is fulfilled we shall return to the Divine spiritual realms of souls, this is the true eternal law of nature and life on earth.

This book Heaven's Register has been written after the overwhelming interest in the website www.heavensregister.com, and although the knowledge is taken from the spiritual Jewish texts, this book is not written for any specific group, race or religion, nor does it contain any rules or man made laws that are specific to the Jewish religion.

Heaven's register is a universal spiritual guide book with keys of knowledge to be used for anyone whose soul pulls them to read this book.

Heaven's Register is a simple spiritual method to enable one to use the power of one's soul, to reconnect with the spirit world from where one soul has come from, thereby connecting with one's guardian angels in order to find one's true destined pathway, enabling one to live a happy, purposeful and fulfilling life in the right place with one's true soulmate.

To all readers we say, there is no order to read this book, we humbly suggest you follow your intuitive instincts, read the chapters that your soul is pulling you to read first, others later and maybe some chapters you will never read until the time is right for you.

Many times you will find all you need to read is a single sentence, and that will be enough your soul needs to read, in order to set your mind thinking and develop your own answers with the spiritual help of your own guardian angels.

I sincerely hope and bless each and every reader to be able to find one's true individualistic and unique pathway to live a fulfilling life, and with the help of one's guardian angels be able to find one's true destined pathway, fulfilling everything that has been planned for one's journey of life in this world as it has been written in the eternal Divine Heavens Register.

Wishing you success and happiness in everything you do every moment of your lives.

# Chapter 2

*"Vocatus atque non vocatus... deus aderit"*
*Called or not called, GOD will be present*
Inscription on Gravestone of
Professor Dr Carl G Jung,
Kusnacht Switzerland

## Belief in GOD and Accepting the Existence of a Soul

### Believing or not believing in a Creator?

Thankfully in our generation we have the freewill choice as to believe or not believe, in the past generations religious leaders brainwashed the population, and in many cases punished with death or violence the non-believers. Hence those irresponsible leaders caused a backlash of rebellion against traditional man-made religious laws and man-made "religions". In our modern day thinking it is unbelievable and inconceivable to understand that anyone can force someone to believe in GOD.

Belief in an eternal Divine Spiritual Creator of the universe and belief in a Spiritual world is a personal experience. It is the part of the journey of life, each and every individual will have their own unique feelings, experiences and beliefs during the course of their lives which will enable one to make one's own conclusions about GOD and the realms of the eternal spiritual world, pure spirituality is about a personal journey to find GOD within one's own soul.

There are three basic spiritual awakenings of the soul that occur during everyone's life, given to help each individual explore a belief in GOD and an existence of a soul.

## 1. Awakening one's soul to believe in GOD

The awakening within one's spiritual soul that there is a great Divine Creator of this infinite universe by looking at the stars in the sky at night and feeling the overwhelming enormity, vastness and greatness of the Creator of this infinite universe.

### שאו מרום עיניכם וראו מי ברא את אלה

"Lift up your eyes towards the heavens, and look ...
Who created these stars?"

Awakening your spiritual soul to see, sense and feel the enormity of the great eternal Divine Creator of the universe.

Throughout the bible, it is suggested for everyone to look at the Moon, the Stars and the Planets in the heavens above at night time. There is something extraordinary spiritual about looking at the beautiful sky on a clear night - especially the radiant moon.

On a clear skied night, just look upwards to the stars in the sky and towards the moon and you will feel a wonderful spiritual energy enter your soul, it is truly amazing, no-one can tell you how or what you will feel, as each person is as unique as each star in the heavens above, but it is guaranteed that you will start to feel something special and unique. From this moment of seeing the image of the stars in the sky your soul will be awakened spiritually.

For thousands of years, millions of people have looked at the stars at night, and have always felt an inexplicable spiritual feeling; people have been recharged spiritually every night by simply looking at the stars in the sky. This energy is as pure and spiritual as the eternal Divine Creator of the universe that created each and every star; this sight of the sky at night is truly a spiritual awakening.

As your eyes are the physical windows of your soul, by looking and connecting to the energy that is emitted from the moon, planets and stars, a spiritual energy of wisdom and understanding is awakened within your soul.

11

The reason a person will start to be awakened to a belief in an eternal Divine Creator of the universe upon seeing the sky at night, is that one will start to think how vast this universe is, and that earth is a small planet moving in the universe totally unsupported in space and yet majestically moving around the sun and spinning on its axis to give us a day and a night. Similarly every planet is moving in space emitting a light and energy at profoundly specific places in the sky at night. Who could possibly have created such an amazing universe? There, quite simply, has to be an eternal Divine Creator, far greater than any human can even imagine – this is the true awakening in a belief in GOD.

## 2. Awakening a belief in the existence of a soul.

The awakening of one's belief in a spiritual soul and a world of souls occurs when someone you love dies and passes over to spirit world. Every single person in the world knows and loves someone, at some stage of their life that dies. This connection known as the overlapping of generations is the essence of the continuity of life that connects all the generations and spirit souls past, present and future.

Belief in the existence of a soul, just like a belief in GOD, is a feeling and awareness that each individual develops for oneself at a destined and specific time.

"The key" that awakens and opens the door in one's mind and thoughts to the existence and belief in a soul is when someone you love or when someone who loves you, dies.

At the moment of death, the person usually gives a few deep gasps of breath and their eyes open wide, suddenly their body comes alive with momentary vitality, they see something with their eyes opened wide, and then they die. Everyone whom has been with someone at the moment of death will tell you the experience is the same. This is "the moment of death experience".

Looking at the body after death, and knowing the person when they where alive, is one of "life's spiritual experiences", it makes everyone think and feel that the body is not just a physical body, but a home to something more - like a soul. Then it arrives - at that moment - an intrinsic belief in some type of life-after-death spirit world and an existence of a soul.

This is the connection of continuity of life. The eternal law of life is that souls come into this physical world at birth and leave the body at death. The soul leaves the physical body and passes over to eternal spirit world of souls, and with the bond of love, one is connected eternally. The stronger the bond of love, the more spiritual the awakening experience within one's soul.

## 3. Awakening the depths of love

The awakening of one's soul when one learns to love. Everyone has within one's soul an infinite wellspring of love. The opening up of true unconditional wellsprings of love within one's soul connects each person directly to the purest of creative energy of this world, a strong connection that makes one fall in love with life and fall in love with love  energy with spiritual love and appreciation for GOD.

Feeling and expressing love, connects one with life energy of GOD. Where there is love there is GOD, and where GOD is there is life, vitality, happiness, faith, hope and peace.

From conception, birth and early childhood, all existence is based on love and the creative life energy of love. This concentration of love, gives the physical and spiritual soul the energy and strength to grow. As a person matures, the natural transition of any normal person is to reverse the role of receiving love into one of giving and creating love energy with one's parents, siblings, friends and family, with genuinely nice people one meets every single day and of course the greatest love of all is with one's true soulmate.

The moment one begins to generate an energy of love is the moment one's soul is awakened. Only an awakened soul can truly love. The wellsprings of love are deep within everyone's soul, once a person has matured and learnt how to love one has then truly mastered the key of life and unlocked a door forever.

When we live with unconditional love, we are filled with life energy and vitality, this feeling of aliveness is like a flowing river of continuous loving Godly life energy. In the same way we were conceived with the LOVE energy of our parents, then throughout all our lives, our vitality and energy is only maintained through the creative LOVE energy we generate each and every day. Without thoughts of love in our lives we are sleeping, only thoughts of love have the power to awaken our soul.

# Where there is LOVE, there is GOD.

# Where there is GOD - there is life, hope, faith and true happiness.

In the book Chovos halevovos Shaar Bechina - ספר חובת הלבבות שער בחינה, known in English as the book "Duties of the Heart" by Rabeinu Yosef Ibn Paquida, teaches that to awaken oneself spiritually especially if one feels tired, lethargic and sleepy during the day, one should immediately focus one's thoughts on love. The greatest and purest love is the love of GOD and love of life.

Thank GOD with love for this opportunity to experience this amazing journey of life on planet earth, with especial thanks for the radiant variety of beautiful colours of the fruits, plants, flowers and trees. For the beauty of the sea, the clouds and rain, sunshine, the stars and the moon in the sky at night, all thoughts of the beauty of nature will generate a real love of life energy within one's soul, and one's soul will truly awaken each and every moment of every day with the energy of love.

At that moment in your life when you feel love in your heart, softening you to become full of love and compassion is the feeling of true spiritual awakening of one's soul.

Once a person has awakened spiritually with love, one's life will never be the same and transformation has just begun. Suddenly one's aims and ambitions change. Life has new meaning with a sense of purpose, enabling a person to explore the meaning of one's life.

# Chapter 3

## Guardian Angels and Individual Spiritual Guidance

### Guardian Angels - Shomrim שׁוֹמרים

כי מלאכיו יצוה לך לשמרך בכל דרכיך

"For He will command His angels to Guard you in all you ways"
Psalms 91 verse 11.

The Spirit world is simply a world of spirit souls that surrounds us, in harmony with this physical world, but on a different vibration. In a similar way that we know the atmosphere around us is full of electromagnetic frequencies of airwaves, anything from television airwaves, radio waves to mobile phone conversations, all those signals are transmitted in the air around us on different levels of frequencies.

These energies exist and yet we cannot see them with our physical eyes, if one has a suitable receiver then one can tune-in to the energies in the air around us. Similarly Spirit souls and Divine energy is all around us vibrating on higher energies and frequencies, if only we knew how to tune-in to the spiritual energies we would know so much!

### Two Guardian Angels

Each and every person is blessed with at least two guardian angels with him/her all the time. This is a spiritual fact, whether one senses them or not, whether one is aware of their presence, they are always there and there purpose is to look after, guide and protect YOU.

The first mention of Guardian Angels accompanying a person in the Bible is in Genesis 28 verse 12, when Jacob rests for the night and sees a transfer of his angels, some leaving him and some joining him, at that moment when he was leaving Israel on a special journey on his own in need of an extra and different kind of protection.

The principle of Guardian Angels is explained more clearly in the Holy Book Tana Devei Eliyahu, written 2000 years ago by Rav Onan and the prophet Elijah Eliyahu.

אם עושה אדם את עצמו צדיק ולדבר אמת

מוסרין לו מלאך שמתנהג עמו בדרך צדיקים ומדבר אמת

The paragraph above is in original Hebrew from Tana Devei Eliyahu Zuta Chapter 3 paragraph 4 .ג פרק זוטא אליהו דבי תנא

To translate: - If a person makes himself to be a righteous person and speak the truth, he is given an Angel who guides him along the path of righteous people and truth is always spoken to him. If a person makes himself to be wicked, to corrupt and speaks lies, then an angel will be attached to him who will corrupt him/her and mislead them in life. If a person makes himself a Chassid - an especially kind and thoughtful person, accepting everything painful, then a special angel is given to the person which can guide along the pathway of the exceedingly righteous, giving them strength to sustain any pain.

To explain in words of my teacher, the Biala Rebbe of Lugano who was taught from his father the Famous Biala Rebbe Chelkas Yehoshua יהושוע חלקת, Rabbi Yehoshua Rabinowitz, who learnt the book "Tana Devei Eliyahu" from memory, whilst in Siberia during the Second World War.

The Biala Rebbe explains, each of us has two guardian angels, similarly to having friends. If you treat your friends nicely then they stay with you, if you lie and cheat your friends, they will go away, and other types of friends will befriend you, probably low life - cheats and liars. If you ignore your friends who are trying to be kind and helpful to you, then they will ignore you.

If however, you move up the social ladder by dressing smartly, talking eloquently, honestly, respectfully and behaving morally then you will automatically attract a much better class of friend, and if you pay attention to and appreciate your friends good advice then they will give you more good advice and guidance, similarly and even more so with our Guardian Angels.

Our thoughts, words and actions have a profound affect on our sensitive Guardian Angels, the major gift we have over the animal kingdom is our ability to speak, hence, this is the judging factor by which our Guardian Angels energies and strength are monitored and given to guide us, all depending on the way we use the power of speech. Lies and deceit are so abhorrent and unacceptable that it induces from spirit world the worst disruptive consequences.

## Be Careful with one's power of SPEECH

כל המספר לשון הרע .... אין לו חלק לעולם הבא

One who speaks gossip, even if it's true, against another loses their right to his/her destiny and destined place in spirit world. Talmud Sanhedrin page 90a.

The spiritual law teaches us that gossiping, telling lies, ruins and corrupts a person soul, so much damage that angels are given to the person, to corrupt their lives even more. As a direct consequence that the person has abused the power of his/her speech through their lies, deceit, slander and gossiping, that the persons prayers are not answered.

Conversely, it makes the ability to change for the better so simple. Just tell the truth, be 100% careful with every word, then good guides and good Guardian Angels will guide and protect you.

The specific energy of planet earth is the number two; everything on earth arrives and comes in PAIRS. Our physical body contains two of everything, we belong in pairs, a male and female exists in every living entity on planet Earth.

Similarly we are given two guardian angels to help balance our soul. These two angels work together to create the energy and opportunities in our life, to guide us to have a purposeful and fulfilling life. One angel gives one the ability to think logically and the other emotionally, a balanced male and female energy from each Angel.

## There are two types of people in this world.

The first and most wonderful category is the HONEST group, which basically means when you are nice to them they are nice in return; when you are horrible to them they are horrible in return. When you ask them a question, you are given the honest answer in return. The intrinsic goodness of this group will always make you feel alive and happy. When you hear something good has happened to anyone of this group, you too - feel the happiness. Conversely when something bad happens you feel their sorrow and pain. The honest group person, will always find ways to be nice and compliment, saying nice constructive words, looking for the goodness in people, and they will always radiate love and happiness, even in the face of adversity. They will always find ways to create loving energy and NEVER steal energy from others by hateful, negative or destructive thoughts, words or actions.

The other group of people in this world are the DECEITFUL (liars) people, which basically means when you are nice to them they are horrible in return; when you are horrible to them they are nice in return. When you ask them a question, you are given lies and deceit in return. The intrinsic deceit and twistedness of this group, will always make you feel drained and sad (unless you are of the same type - in which case you feel re-assured and happy mixing with them, as you will always end up gossiping and slandering good people, and re-assuring yourselves that your lifestyle is the correct one ). When you hear something good has happened to anyone of this group - you feel a sadness or indifferent, or when something bad happens to this group, you either feel happy or indifferent. That is to say, the soulful energy is not exuded or radiated from this type of person; they are usually very closed and selfish with their energies.

The good thing about being in the honest group is that in a short time of speaking to the other deceitful group, you instinctively know who they are, your guides and angelic helpers, give you the feeling. And in the conversation with them, they lie or contradict themselves and you catch them out. This is the protection given to you by GOD and your Guardian Angels.

A deceitful person will always lie, they cannot help themselves, it is natural for them. They are always caught out by the honest group of people. There will always be signs along the way, they may cheat of their husbands/wives, at work they will be lazy, sleeping on the job or time wasting etc., or as bosses they will abuse their staff and never show appreciation, continue cheating and fiddling their staff out of money, basically they have no morals or ethical standards, and they don't trust anyone because they themselves are not to be trusted.

# Attracting Good Guardian Angels

This ability to categorize the two groups is directly related to this subject of Guardian Angels, as it is intrinsically important and establishes the foundations of spiritual law that enables good guardian angels to attach themselves to one's soul for good spiritual growth, and thereby releasing the deceitful and misleading angels.

Therefore, be careful of every word you speak, knowing that the words you use will have an affect on your spiritual guardian angels. By using the correct words in your life you will improve yourself spiritually and thereby be worthy of extra guardian angels whom will attach themselves to you and your soul, to enhance your life on a pathway of spiritual growth. The freewill choice is yours.

**In the way you wish to go in life, so you will be led by your Guardian Angels**

בדבר או שיחוודע הדבר פ״י קרובים ופמולים שפמור הגואל אם יכרגנו הרי״ק : בדרך אהבה רבה

This printed passage above is from the famous Rabbi Edels (who lived 1555 – 1631) known as the MAHARSHA מהרשא from the Talmud Makkos page 10b.

This passage explains that, "in the way you wish to go in life, so you will be led by your Guardian Angels". The Maharsha Rabbi Shlome Edels explains, that every action, word and thought that you do in this world creates an angel, so if you really want something good to happen in your life, create enough angelic good angels with kindness, loving thoughts and honest words. Then these angels you have attracted to you by your good thoughts, words and actions will indeed lead you to your goal

## Two Angels

Reb Chaim Vital in the Book Otzrus Hachaim אוצרות החיים and Shaar Kavonus שער כוונות written 440 years ago explains the principle that everything in this world occurs in pairs, you are were born with two Guardian Angels who are appointed from birth to guide you along you destined way in life, to ensure you follow your life's pathway. Their duty is to make sure you do not miss any of your destined meetings or encounters in life. And to make sure you find your destined soulmate partner, have their success in your job / career which will provide money to support your life and you will be able to fulfill your purpose of life to your maximum potential.

Certain major destined goalposts are set out in our life, it depends on us if we meet them, or get side-tracked, or if we have detached ourselves and ignored messages and guidance from our Guardian Angels. If this is the case then when we wake-up spiritually at any moment or time in our life, then our Guardian Angels will always be there for us, and thereby always help us to find our way back to our destined true pathway in life.

Above your two guardian angels is third angel known as a "gate keeper" angel, שׁוֹמֵר פתחים who monitors the energy around you, allowing in and out, the good and not good angels to help you or distract you according to your efforts.

Immediately we must write - to say that a "not good" angel does not exist, it is in fact a challenging and good Angel that is created by one's misdeeds, lies and dishonesty, and is their to corrupt and make a persons life unsuccessful and unhappy until one WAKES up, to change and return to the true destined pathway, much like a strict disciplined teacher.

# Chapter 4

## Communicating with your Guardian Angels

According to the principle that NOTHING in this world happens by accident, every single event in your life happens for a specific reason guided from spirit world השגחה פרטית . Reb Chaim Vital explains the fact that a person is attracted to read his books on Guardian Angels, especially Sefer Gilgulim - the Book of Reincarnation of souls, then this means that your soul is thirsty and prepared to learn.

Similarly if you have found this book "Heavens Register" and are reading this chapter it means that YOU are now ready to learn how to communicate with your spiritual guardian angels, and most importantly you have been guided to read this chapter at this moment, and they are waiting to communicate with you.

Reb Chaim Vital explains that there is no need to exert any effort to connect with them, it will happen at the correct time for your soul, and now is that time for you. It depends on your spiritual level and not on your physical age.

The awakening in your spiritual life will happen in a dream or a strange coincidence, where you will feel a special inexplicable spiritual feeling, that there is more to life, other than what appears to the physical eye and to logic. You may still have free choice to ignore these signs, be closed and pretend to yourself that there is no such thing as Guardian Angels; however they are around you NOW, and watching over you as you are reading this chapter in this book, they are your Guardian Angels and there duty is to look after, guide and protect you during your whole life on earth.

As you think about them, and even start to talk to them as if they are really with you, you will start to feel the special peaceful loving and re-assuring energy, it is inexplicable, as each person senses this differently, but I assure you - you will feel it.

Once you have started this communication and connection with them, other good spiritual guides and angels will come into your aura and give you the knowledge and spiritual feelings as you need as you are progressing along your journey.

## Light a Candle

Lighting a single white candle and saying one's prayers is extremely spiritual. A candle is symbolic of the soul, a material physical candle burns with a lovely peaceful glow and energy, turning itself into light and warmth, as the physical candle burns it disappears into the air, the energy into the ether, so too - the soul as it passes away from this world, no longer needs a physical body.

This is the spiritual reason why candles are used for remembering spirit souls, a solid physical candle turning itself into warmth and light as it burns away, with nothing physically remaining. In the same way a candle transforms and changes so too, a person's soul leaves this physical world and enters Spirit world with peace, love and light.

Lighting a candle announces to the spirit world and to one's spiritual Guardian Angels that one wishes to connect to the eternal spirit world and pray.

## Simply Talk to Your Guardian Angels with Honesty

Talk to your Guardian Angels regularly, tell them how you feel, the more you develope spiritually and sensitively, the more you will know by yourself what to say, the intuitive thoughts will come into your mind and soul instinctively.

Always start your conversation by THANKING your Guardian Angels for the help they have given you each and every day in looking after you. Then you are indeed ready to ask them for a sign, and guidance according to your needs each and everyday.

Reb Chaim Vital emphasizes the importance of honesty, kindness, and being 100% careful with the power of your speech, will indeed assure you of good angels whom will instruct you along the good kind and truly honest spiritual pathway. If you talk silly and superficial things with your Guardian Angels you can only expect them to take you as a superficial and childish too! Grow up and be mature, ask for help and guidance realistically, it's not a game!

**Guardian Angels are always there even if you don't feel their presence**

One night a man had a dream. He dreamed he was walking along the beach with his Guardian Angel. Across the sky flashed scenes from his life. For each scene, he noticed two sets of footprints in the sand; one belonging to him and the other to his Guardian Angel.

When the last scene of his life flashed before him, he looked back at the footprints in the sand. He noticed that many times along the path of his life there was only one set of footprints. He also noticed that it happened at the very lowest and saddest times in his life.

This really bothered him and he questioned his Guardian Angel about it. "Guardian Angel, you said that once I decided to recognize your existence and listen to you, you'd walk with me all the way. But I have noticed that during the most troublesome times in my life, there is only one set of footprints. I don't understand why when I needed you most you would leave me."

The Guardian Angel replied, "My precious child, I Love you and would never leave you. During your times of trial and suffering, when you see only one set of footprints, it was then that I carried you."

**Extra Special Spiritual Times to Communicate with one's Guardian Angels**

According to tradition, there are indeed more opportune moments to connect spiritually. On the yarzheit, that is the anniversary of death, of a loved one passing to spirit world, are exceedingly strong days spiritually to pray and connect with them, according to jewish tradition we light at least two candles, one for their soul and one for yours, and one will feel a special spirituality in one's life on those specific days.

Another especially good time is Friday evening, lighting candles at sunset to commence the Sabbath-the day of spiritual recharging. This time applies to all of humanity, Friday evening, is indeed a spiritual evening in the whole world for everyone (both Moslems who go to Mosque on Friday's and Christians who eat fish and not meat on Friday's).

The reason is that Friday has always been the end of the physical working week, a transference takes place of Physical energy at the end of the working week on Friday becoming Spiritual energy at sunset on Friday evening each and every single week.

Those people who go out to get drunk, discos or parties, or even those people who waste time and watch TV or go to bed early on Friday evening are missing a great opportunity to grow spiritually every single week on the Friday evening. Try and change for just one Friday evening, light candles and think spiritually, you will be amazed at the affect it will have on the whole of the following week.

This spiritual gift to all of humanity is that on the Friday evening at sunset each person is given an extra Guardian Angelic, נשמה יתירה Angel, according to what he/she deserves by his/her actions during that week.

# Making Your Own Spiritual Time

The best way to connect to spirit world is to visit the graves of good righteous people you have known in your life. The gravesite is the last physical connection they had on earth and therefore the beginning of their spiritual spirit world journey. The presence of their spirit soul at their gravesite can be attracted there when you visit.

Their soul will then be able to infuse a spiritual energy within you, of knowledge and understanding, and they will guide you. They will NOT force you to do anything, you have freewill choice, but they will give you the intuition and knowledge you need to know the difference between right and wrong pathway.

## Keep It Secret

Reb Chaim Vital makes an important point, and this is exceedingly important, and that is DO NOT TELL ANYONE about your spiritual experiences, they are private between you and your Guardian Angels and GOD.

We have known many people who had the spiritual potential but by telling their cynically dishonest parents, family or so-called non-spiritual friends, their energies were strong enough to block this sensitive spiritual link. Their journey to spiritual success took a longer more painful detour, as they had to overcome the negative thoughts and words of non-believing destructive people. Nonetheless that is also destiny as some people love to learn the hardest and most painful way possible. Your Guardian Angel will tell you when it is time and with whom it is safe to talk about these spiritual matters.

## Listen Carefully to your Inner Voice and to Your Guardian Angels

As you are beginning your spiritual journey the basic fundamental key you need, is your connection with your guardian angels, it must be honest, trustworthy and strong, with a basis and a focused purpose of selfless service to GOD and to spirit world.

Your Guardian Angels communicate to you through your soul, the talk to you through your own inner voice, and through implanting good ideas in your mind, thoughts and soul. They also give you good or bad feelings about something or someone. Listen and react according to how they make you feel. Only by acting on their advice successfully or being saved from a bad situation will you start to believe in their comforting guiding and protective presence in your life.

Know and believe that your Guardian Angels are always with you and will always love you. They are on your side and will always want to help you, no matter how many opponents or difficulties you may have in life. Your guardian angels will try and help you as much as they possibly can; they do this out of love for you and desire to help you maximize your spiritual potential in life.

Always remember to thank GOD, spirit world and your guardian angels for the help you receive every moment of every day of your life.

# Chapter 5

## The Puzzle of Life; How to Find
## Ones True Destiny and Pathway

ארבעים יום קודם יצירת הולד בת קול יוצאת ואומרת
פלוני לפלוני בית פלוני לפלוני שדה פלוני לפלוני בת

"Forty days before a person is conceived into this world, it is announced in heaven's register in the eternal Divine spirit world, the daughter of this man is destined to marry this man, the house in this place is destined for their home, and this field (livelihood / business / profession) is destined for this person". Talmud Sota 2a

### It's all written in Heavens Register - Destiny has been declared

All one needs to do is trust in GOD, pray and trust in one's Guardian Angels that one will be guided to one's true destined life, with the right soulmate at the right time and in the right place.

### The Two Spiritual Rules of "Destiny" on Earth

**1.** Every living person on earth is only a half of one whole; everyone has someone special, one's true loving soulmate; all one needs to do is find one's soulmate to be wholesome and complete. Every living unit on earth has a female and a male; they are not two separate individuals, they are each a half of a whole.

Once one has found one piece of the puzzle of one's destiny, all the other pieces will come together magically, so either focus on finding one's true soulmate, one's destined purpose in life, one's livelihood or finding one's home, the best place for one to live and then the other pieces of destiny will simply happen "magically".

**2.** If one has gone astray from one's original destiny, there is a Divine spiritual guarantee that one can always come back to one's true pathway, with the help of one's Guardian Angels.

Simply light 2 candles for one's Guardian Angels and ask them to help you to find your true destined pathway, ask for signs and guidance, and listen intuitively to the answers and suggestions one's Guardian Angels will put in one's mind thoughts and soul.

Do this for 30 days and one will start to feel one is being put back onto one's true pathway; if one continues praying and asking one's guardian angels every day then within 12 months one will actually be with one's true soulmate, in the right place with all the right destined pieces of one's life.

**The True Soulmate**

The spiritual and physical energy of planet earth resonates to the number two; everything on our planet comes in pairs. The emphasis and importance of finding one's true soulmate is the key to success in life on earth. Having the "wrong half" means one does not have the right key to fulfill one's true destined purpose in life. Without the right "key", one's life will seem frustrating and unlucky, like stuck in a locked room full of closed doors. It maybe nice few hours, but would be frustratingly painful to remain there for the rest of one's life!

**Everyone has a perfect destined Soulmate**

This is an important fact, as one needs to firmly believe that every person has a perfect destined loving soulmate. Never give up hope, and never attempt to steal someone else's soulmate, be relaxed about finding one's soulmate then he / she will come into one's life quicker than one can even imagine !

**Destiny is Written in the Astrology of the Stars and in Palms of Ones Hands**

The study of Astrology and wisdom of Palmistry will explain that destiny is mapped out for everyone. All the gifts and energy you need to make a perfect journey in your life are given to you, so that you can maximize your true potential, and fulfill your soul's specific and purpose in this physical journey we call life.

Everyone has a way, unique to their astrological character to earn a living, communicate with people, get married and live a purposeful and creative life of love. As we explain in the chapter Wisdom of Palmistry that everyone's hands have at least one marriage line next to the heart line, this simply gives proof that everyone has been blessed with at least one potential soulmate.

## Belief in "Destiny" - Trusting in GOD and spirit world

## Summary of "Destiny"

The basic spiritual rule of destiny is that life is a journey from childhood to adulthood, learning to transform from a taker into a giver and creator of loving energy.

We pray that, as "Destiny" assures everyone with Divine help and help from one's Guardian Angels, the records in Heaven's Register will be fulfilled, and everyone will live a happy, purposeful life with one's true soulmate. No one on earth should ever be alone, that is simply not the purpose nor the will of GOD for life on an "Earth of pairs".

# Chapter 6

## Understanding How to Find Ones True SOULMATE

In this chapter we shall explain the meaning of soulmates and how to find and identify one's true soulmate, taken from Sefer Shinuyim - the Book of Changes.

### 1. The Purpose and Meaning of Soulmates and Soul Groups.

The true purpose of the gift of life on earth is in order for our souls to learn and experience life, through all kinds of events, opportunities and challenges throughout our lives.

Thankfully we are not alone during our journey of life, unless of course a person believes themselves to be selfish egocentrical individuals, then even amongst large groups of people they are lonely and disconnected.

### The Soulgroup

During our journey of life, we travel on this earth in soul groups that is a group, culture and identity where all the members of the soul group understand each other and live on the same physical and spiritual wavelength. The members of one's soul group may not all be alive on earth, they may be spiritual souls who have passed onto to Spirit world but maintain contact with you as they are part of one's soul group in much the same way as Guardian Angels.

One will always be able to rely upon one's soul group to help, guide, assist, the souls in one's soul group will make 100% certain that one succeeds to fulfill ALL of one's life's goals, objectives, challenges and purpose one's soul came to earth to learn.

Once a person has learnt the lessons of one's life, it is possible to elevate one's soul into a higher soulgroup, and likewise if one makes a bad decision one can move out of one's soulgroup into a lower group. Nonetheless one always has the intrinsic continual opportunity and chance to return to one's destined soulgroup and likewise on is always guaranteed to be able to find their perfect soulmate, through the help of one's Guardian Angels and helpful souls from one's soulgroup.

## The Soulmate

As we explained in the previous chapter in the puzzle of life teaches that destiny has designated each and every individual with a soulmate. The soulmate is actually the other half of a person. With one's soulmate one is wholesome, without it one is void and empty.

The spiritual and physical energy of planet earth resonates to the number two; everything on our planet comes in pairs. The Earth itself is paired with the Moon, the identity of the Earth needs the Moon to exist both physically and spiritually, in the renewal of energies monthly and daily tidal flows, as the magnetic pull of the Moons energy causes high and low tides - the Earth needs change to exist.

The emphasis and importance of finding one's true soulmate is the key to success in life. The two halves that make the whole, once together one can lead a fulfilling and destined purposeful life. Having the wrong half means one does not have one's soulmate hence one does not have the key of life to fulfill one's true destined purpose in life.

Without the right key, one's life will seem frustrating and unlucky - like stuck in a locked room full of closed doors. It maybe nice for a few hours, but would be frustratingly painful to remain there for the rest of one's life!

The purpose of the soulmate is to make a person feel wholesome with love and enable one to accomplish the mission and purpose of life through physical, sexual and spiritual love energy. Everything constructive and good in this life is only created through love, only through the loving energy created together with one's soulmate creates the perfect energy to live, bringing meaning to everything in one's life.

## 2. Explaining that everyone has 2 potential Soulmates, עזר כנגדו ,

### One is a help עזר, the other is a challenging opposition כנגדו.

Everyone has freewill choice in life, even when we think we are making a choice, it is either categorized into a good decision or a bad decision. Both decisions are choices that are potentially destined for our soul, the bad decisions we make will challenge us and make life difficult for us in order to guide us to change, making the corrective decision and finding the correct good pathway, our soul instinctively only finds "inner peace of mind", when we are on the correct pathway.

Most people only learn from bad and challenging relationships. Such connections will have a similar instantaneous magnetic attraction as good relationships, as they too, are destined in order to teach a person important lessons, but they will continue to repeat past patterns if bad relationships as there is a lesson a person needs to learn, and until one learns the lesson one will keep on being magnetic to the bad and challenging type of relationships.

### The 2 Types of Soulmates "עזר - The Help"

"עזר - The Help" soulmates are always 100% on your side with continual support, help, love, passion and an eternal unconditional love, and whom would never ever hurt you.

Whenever one plans, talks and thinks ideas with one's true helpful soulmate, they constructively help to energize one's life with loving energy, enabling one to overcome any negativity, moving all obstacles and finding the correct pathway to success. As one's true helpful soulmate always knows that they are one's other half, when something good happens to the other half of them, they too benefit from this good energy.

## "כנגדו - The Opposition"

"כנגדו - The Opposition" soulmates teach a person by constantly challenging, through emotionally bitter lessons with pain and difficulties. The opposition bad relationships always cause sensible people to go closed on themselves emotionally in order to protect their soul.

In such a dysfunctional relationship people prefer to live alone in one's mind and thoughts than communicate with such a destructive person. A feeling of living with the enemy ensues, and everything one plans or tells such a person gets blocked and thwarted by their destructive and negative thought energies, critical words and horrible actions.

Until it comes a point in one's life, where one says "ENOUGH"! At such a breaking point a person may loose faith in love, loose faith in relationships, loose faith life and worst of all - loose faith in GOD.

But when a person realizes that such a relationship was and is a dysfunctional "כנגדו - Opposition" soulmate, then this makes a person find an inner strength, admitting to oneself the truth of the bad relationship and then learning how to find one's true 100% loving soulmate the soulmate of "עזר - Help".

## "עזר - The Help" can sometimes be a "כנגדו - The Opposition"

There are times that we all make mistakes in our lives, and even though we are living with and have found our 100% loving soulmate, he/she may challenge us and be absolutely right to challenge with the strength of opposition.

They act in this way of challenging opposition as they are wishing to defend their own soul, through love of their other half of their soul; they are trying to protect the relationship from any destructive external opposing energy and any negative influence or bad decision the other person has made. They are challenging and opposing out of a deep sincere love, in order to protect the wholesomeness of their perfect soulmate union.

**"כנגדו - The Opposition" can sometimes turn into "עזר - The Help"**

"כנגדו - The Opposition" soulmates always have the potential to become perfectly 100% loving soulmates, with no more need for bitter experiences, pain or difficulties only when they have refined and elevated their soul after learning the necessary lessons their souls need to learn.

Soulmates may choose to start their relationship through a challenging and opposing energy, however, by working together and challenging each others individualism they are able to transform themselves into a single united soulmate, through negating any opposing energies that exist by learning to completely love each other, and thereby transform their relationship into a 100% loving helpful soulmate union.

## 3. How to Find Ones True Soulmate

When meeting new people in life, connections and bonds are made either because the people share a common interest or because one person has something the other person wants.

**Physical Chemistry**

In the case of love and relationships, men and women are magnetically aroused and attracted to each other. Nonetheless not all men are attracted to all women and vice versa, there needs to be a certain chemistry that makes a man and a woman fall in love with each other.

This chemistry is the energy of the thoughts in the mind, that is a man and a woman only really feel a connection to each other when they are in harmony with each other in their mind & thoughts. This common factor enables a wholesomeness and fullness in the relationship; otherwise the love is merely a superficial animal - instinct sexual love, which usually fades within a few weeks.

Human beings who are connected with each other, need to have an ability to think the same way as each other, they need to have a common factor in order to feel the relationship is wholesome. Hence the reason why single people join clubs and organizations, or have hobbies and interests as a sense of identity of their personality. Thereby enabling them to meet like-minded people and hopefully find a suitable man/woman with whom they can have a meaningful relationship with, as their inner minds and thoughts will be sharing similar identities, emotions and feelings.

If either become disinterested in the common factor that originally united them, then their relationship will have communication problems leading to an automatic falling out of love, as their thoughts and energy of their minds no longer have anything in common.

When a couple is not growing together, then they are growing apart in their diverging lifestyles and interests. Such a relationship will eventually fail completely, unless one of them changes to become like the other.

## Spiritual Chemistry

The next level of relationships is that people feel a magnetic attraction, a twinkle in the eye or very lovely inner feeling, even without talking. Relationships that are prompted by just a thought of them, seeing them or seeing anything that reminds you of them, that is your mind and soul is connecting yourself with their mind and thoughts.

Such thought energies are one's mind and soul communicating with you and likewise with the other persons mind and soul is feeling the same inner feeling for you, your souls are communicating with each other, this gives you the inner spiritual feeling that you are made for each other, an inexplicable inner spiritual chemistry.

Such a spiritual chemistry is definitely a sign that this is someone important in your life and definitely from one's soulgroup. The important question how do you identify if they are your true soulmate? This needs you to understand the concept of soulmate chemistry:-

## Soulmate Chemistry

Soulmates and all members of one's soulgroup have a unique telepathic communication of thought energies in the minds and souls of the whole soulgroup. All the souls of one's soulgroup know and sense exactly what the other members are feeling. They all have the same thoughts, feelings and emotions at the same time. They feel pain, when people in their soulgroup are in pain, and likewise they feel the happiness, love and strength from the other souls in their soulgroup.

The soulmate chemistry means that all the souls of the soulgroup are constantly connected even if they are physically far away from each other, they are very close spiritually, as their soul, mind and thoughts are constantly connected.

This soulmate chemistry is the reason why one's Guardian Angels and loved one's in spirit world, are in constant contact with one's soul, as they are members of one's spiritual soul group. The only reason a person feels alone and not in contact with people of their same soulgroup is because one may block or deny the existence of spirit world, believing that one needs to get on with normal physical life instead of including a spiritual enlightened pathway within one's physical existence in this life on earth.

## How to Find Your True Soulmate

The first step in finding your true soulmate is to believe in GOD, Spirit world, Guardian Angels and that through your connection to good souls in the eternal Divine Spirit world from your soulgroup, you will be guided to find your soulmate or that your soulmate will find you.

## Asking for Guidance for Ones Soul

Sefer Tikunim in the section "Correcting one's soul", Tikun Neshoma תיקון נשמה explains when a person has lived a life void of any belief in GOD, belief in spiritual afterlife or in a Spirit World of Souls, then a person should light 3 candles to connect spiritually:-

37

One candle for GOD, one candle for one's guardian angel and one candle for one's soul, and then pray that one should be guided spiritually to correct any mistakes one has made whilst living a life void of any belief in GOD, and ask to be guided along the right pathway destined for one's soul.

Whilst praying one will feel spiritually enlightened, with feelings of awareness and belief in GOD and belief in the existence of a spiritual soul, such feelings and understandings will bring a person to see a bigger picture, that life on earth is part of a spiritual journey for one's soul, with a unique and destined pathway for each and every soul to experience emotions, events and changes.

**Connecting to Spirit World With Prayer Will Help to Strengthen Your Soul and Enable Your Soulmate to be Found and Bring You Together.**

Every prayer helps to connect one's soul to Spirit world and brings a person closer to the DIVINE GOD that creates and sustains this Universe.

All connections to Spirit World will increase and strengthen your spiritual strength, this includes praying at the gravesites of spiritually strong and good souls, especially praying at the gravesites of good people one knew and loved, and/or praying at Famous Rabbis & Rebbes holy gravesites, sending prayer requests into the famous Rabbi Yonatan Ben Uziel ( see www.uziel.info ) and of course continually giving thanks for the gift of life whilst asking for help and guidance to find one's true soulmate.

One should use one's own language to pray from one's heart for one's soulmate with a few heartfelt emotions and tears. It does not matter what time of the day or night, even if one wakes up in the middle of the night, say a prayer, whenever one intuitively and spiritually feels the right moment to pray and ask for spiritual help, then light a candle and pray in whatever language you understand. The stronger one's inner spiritual connection the sooner one's true soulmate will be found by spirit world and you will come together.

# Lighting Candles For Your Soulmate

## Light 2 Candles: One for You and One for Your Soulmate

In preparing for your soulmate to come into your life, you will develope a selfless and spiritual character, by lighting a candle for the soul of your soulmate even though you have not met him/her yet, you are showing a love, compassion and desire to pray and help someone else, who is actually YOUR other half.

Learning to show love, desiring to give selflessly and unconditionally to another person is all part of growing-up from being a selfish child into a loving perfect potential parent.

Ask yourself, "would you give EVERYTHING of what you have to your soulmate?" if the answer is "YES", then you have understood that giving to your soulmate is infact just giving to yourself, a cycle of life energy. The concept of sharing and giving love in a soulmate loving relationship is the spiritual basis of life, as in the cycle of life in the whole Universe; the DIVINE GOD constantly gives everything to everyone.

When praying for one's soulmate, never focus your thoughts on any particular person, as they may not be yours, and an even better person will be your destined perfect soulmate, and then be open to listen to your inner voice of guidance and ACT, there is no point in praying and then DOING NOTHING when one has a feeling to go somewhere or speak to someone!

## Within 12 Months

The Spiritual guarantee from Sefer Shinuyim - Book of Changes and from famous Rabbi Yonatan Ben Uziel is that within 12 months of prayers of asking GOD and Spirit world to find one's true soulmate then one will find him/her, DIVINE coincidences, experiences and feelings will occur to guide you to your soulmate and guide your soulmate to you.

## Compare to Modern Day Internet

If one is searching for someone on the internet then one first needs to get a computer and be online, then a person needs to search by using a search engines like Google or Yahoo.

Similarly spiritually, in searching for one's true soulmate, one first needs to believe in GOD and Spirit world, connecting by way of prayers and lighting candles for GOD and Spirit world for DIVINE help to find one's soulmate, and then be open, listen and allow one to be guided to meet one's soulmate.

Everyone has a perfect soulmate and when you find him/her your soul will instinctively know, your life will magically open up with an amazing life vitality of love and life-giving energy.

With your true soulmate you will feel an eternal love energy, as soulmates existed in spirit world before we were born when our souls arrived on earth and will exist unified together once we die and leave this earth. The intermediary years of life on earth is the challenge that we must ensure we waste no time in finding our true soulmate to live a wholesome purposeful loving life together.

## The True Soulmate

"One who looks for money, beauty, status or anything physical in a relationship will never find their true soulmate". In seeking your true Soulmate ask yourself the following questions:-

When contemplating one's emotions with respect to one's true soulmate, one needs to ask do you want to be so different from that person OR do you wish to actually be identical to that person, and be a part of that person, in every single way?

In the desire to be that person, and become a complete part of that person's life because indeed a true soulmate is the other half, one is motivated and prepared to change one's mind, thoughts and even physical existence to be with him/her, energized by a magnetic love from the soul.

This power from one's soul is an identity that indicates one's true soulmate, the desire to reunite your souls together as one in this world as you have been before you came into this world and will be united eternally in spirit world after leaving this physical life for eternity, and refusing to allow anything physical or material distract or block your souls from being together. One will not find true inner peace of mind within one's mind and soul until one is with one's true soulmate.

## 4. Explaining the Reason for the Amazing Inexplicable Magnetic Attraction of Soulmates.

In this section we explain the spiritual reason for the amazing inexplicable magnetic attraction of soulmates, and why one feels, senses and knows everything one's soulmate is thinking and feeling.

### Instantaneous Magnetic Attraction

Soulmates have an instantaneous magnetic attraction to each other, as their relationship is blessed by DIVINE GOD, blessed by Spirit world and is destined for them to live their lives together on earth.

Even people who try and fight this magnetic soulmate love desire for each other, will find their efforts to block themselves futile and will eventually be together. As soulmates will never find a peace of mind within their souls until they are together, both physically and spiritually together. True soulmates always need and lovingly enjoy being together all the time.

The reason for this inexplicable magnetic attraction between soulmates is that their Guardian Angels are guiding them and bringing energy to both people simultaneously, in order to force, guide and bring this soulmate couple together. Of course selfish ego, stubbornness and freewill choice can block this, but eventually soulmates always come together. Each persons Guardian Angels will ensure this happens, however illogical!

## Wrong Relationships Always Fail

Similarly, the reason why wrong relationships, lovers and marriages fail is that each of the individuals Guardian Angels are conflicting with the other persons Guardian Angels, both individuals are incompatible on a spiritual level and hence eventually they end up conflicting on a physical level.

A sign for this is that there are conflicts, disharmony and imbalances in the relationship and very often a person enjoys having "space" away from the other, and in the space a person feels enlivened and happy for this freedom! This requirement for space is a sign from one's Guardian Angels to pull one away from a bad and wrong relationship.

Once the wrong person is out of one's life, good fortune and creativity always happens in a persons life, as a spiritual sign from one's Guardian Angels that one is now on the correct pathway and free from that negative person.

Everyone believes in "SIGNS" as these give everyone an indication of good energy, a good omen to one's soul which is living in this real physical world that one is with the right person doing the right thing at the right time. If one feels uncomfortable or misfortune happens where it has not happened before, then take this as a sign and have closure and please run away from them!!!

Once one has closure from draining people, a positive energy of excitement and aliveness is given by one's Guardian Angels, this is because one's soul is blocking success when one is with the wrong people. The more spiritual and sensitive a person is, the stronger the blocking energy is caused by the wrong people in one's life and hence one's Guardian Angels are giving the strongest possible sign to protect you.

## Soulmates Communicate by "Eye Contact"

אסור לאדם לקדש את האשה עד שיראנה
לרעך כמוך שנאמר ואהבת

The Talmud Kiddushin 41a explains that a person is forbidden to marry blindly, unless they see each other with their eyes. The Talmud does not say talk to each other or kiss etc., but the Talmud says a person needs to "to see" with one's eyes.

This is because one's eyes are the windows to one's soul, and "eye contact" means that your souls are communicating with each other. Only by "eye contact" will you know that this person is your soulmate and only through your continual "eye contact" your souls are communicating with each other. May you be blessed to find and communicate with your soulmate every moment of every day of your lives.

# Chapter 7

## A Life of LOVE

### 1. Introduction "What is LOVE?"

Love is the most amazing inexplicable feeling and emotion that we can ever sense with our physical body. Love energy brings life vitality, strength, courage and a desire to want to live life to the fullest potential.

Love is the collective and common energy that connects each person to each other in the whole world. It connects our physical body with the spiritual soul, to the Spirit world and to GOD.

Love is the emotion that is sensed through the senses of sight, smell, sound, taste, touch. The highest form of Love is sensed directly within our soul from other souls and from spirit world.

Love is an energy that can only be fully felt when it is shared with other people. It is impossible to contain Love energy selfishly for oneself, (that is why selfish people cannot find true love), the only way to feel love energy in one's life is when one connects with other people, with spirit world and with GOD, with love.

Love gives life and is the meaning of life. When one has LOVE one has everything, without LOVE one has nothing. Pure Love is a spiritual energy and therefore is always completely FREE, no one can buy true love, synthetic and superficial love always costs money!

The creative life energy of this world is GOD, and GOD is LOVE, LOVE creates life, LOVE sustains life, and the lack of love or hate means death.

## The Heart Beats for Love

The heart is physical centre of one's emotions especially of LOVE energy. Whenever one feels the energy of love one's heart starts to beat

faster. The faster one's heart beats the more emotional energy one senses, until one feels the overwhelming loving energy that takes one's breath away.

Whenever a person finds their heart beating faster this is a sign that one is receiving energy of LOVE. Whether it is a physical attraction of love or a spiritual energy of love or someone's loving thoughts who are thinking of you, this is indicated by a persons heart beating faster in excitement.

The sense of anticipation in most peoples life is felt by one's heart beating faster, the secret is to recognize that this energy is not trying to overwhelm or make a person panic but it is a gift of love energy into one's soul, and one should appreciate this energy and use it wisely sharing it selflessly to love people. Just remember to take a deep breathe, don't feel anxious and enjoy whatever is going to happen in one's life, now that one has this energy of love.

Remember the purpose of this overwhelming excitable love energy indicated by faster heart-beat is in order for one to desire to give love and share this love selflessly with someone else. Pure love energy is only truly felt when sharing with other people, love can never be hoarded and kept for one's self, as this blocks the flow of more love energy coming into one's life.

Sadly, many people find love energy too overwhelming and try to find ways to suppress such love emotions, by drinking alcohol, smoking cigarettes etc , but once a person learns to handle this energy one can have an amazingly energized life of LOVE. So NEVER block or suppress such lovely emotions when one finds one's heart beating faster, simply take a few deep breathes and learn to LOVE.

## The Beginning of Life is LOVE

Every single physical living entity in the whole world is created from love. Even hateful and depressed parents have a moment excitable overwhelming love energy, when they "make love", when their hearts beat fast full of LOVE, that is needed in order to create a child.

## The Reason for Living Life is to LOVE

"שנים של שנאה יפה שעה אחת של אהבה יותר מאלף"

"One moment of love gives more life and is worth more than a 1000 years of hate"

Life is about the moments of excitement when you truly love; those loving moments are the true energy of creative life energy. The more moments of true selfless love one has then, the more exciting and enjoyable a person's life is and the aliveness a person feels within their soul. True love is actually connecting one's soul with the eternal DIVINE energy of life from Spirit world and bringing down a יניקה מלמעלה, a life sustaining energy from the realms of Spirit world.

Life is not about the number of breathes you take during your life, but about the amount of moments that take your breath away.

People who never want to love are dead; the only emotion that connects our physical existence to our spiritual soul and connects to the DIVINE source of all energy is love which is love emotions from the heart - all the fast heartbeats of LOVE.

## Love Blockage and Depression

When people block and refuse to allow love energy into their lives they are blocking their own life-energy (יניקה מלמעלה) and committing spiritual suicide, even if by some good fortune of Divine intervention they suddenly are given a chance to love, they find that the overwhelming sense of love is too much for their depressed soul to handle.

Depressed people prefer to thwart, mess up opportunities to love and block their own lives through their bad attitude, preferring to be lonely and depressed without love, than overwhelmed with an aliveness of love energy, so they act to self-destroy any opportunities of love in their lives, which may even cause them to miss their own soulmate, so remember NEVER block or suppress any emotions of the heart.

## 2. Understanding the difference between Physical Love and Spiritual Love

### Physical Love

Every person, every place and in fact every single object in this physical world contains an energy of love. Every single entity in this world has been created with a unique specific type of love energy.

### Spiritual Love & Physical Love

Physical energy is temporary and last for only a short time, hence physical love energy never lasts. In the same way we are only physically alive for a short period of time, similarly physical love is temporary, for example, the physical skin deep beauty of most woman only lasts between 15 to 35 years from when a woman matures, unlike the spiritual beauty, which is radiated from a good, sweet, kind, spiritually-minded woman with a love that lasts for eternity.

Spiritual energy lasts forever and for eternity, as it communicates and embeds itself within our soul, such eternal emotional true love is carried over from previous lifetimes and carried onwards to future reincarnations. This explains the inexplicable love connection of soulmates which lasts forever.

### How to Make Love Last Forever

In order to make anything last forever, it must be SPIRITUAL, and its energy needs to have made an indelible mark on one's mind, thoughts and soul. Anything that only has a physical energy will fade away and die.

In order to create a LOVE that will last forever, it must be energized with a spiritual emotional LOVE energy, through reasoning, feelings and emotions from one's mind, thoughts and soul.

Imagine that you only have 10 seconds left in your life to see, whatever you see in these 10 seconds will stay with your soul forever, by sensing an urgency of time this sometimes wakes a person up spiritually, then one's heart will start to beat faster with an excitement and a desire to live a loving life, which gives such energy that makes it irreversibly impossible for a person to ever feel depressed and unloved again.

**Learn to Forgive**

סדר קריאת שמע על המטה

רבונו על עולם. הריני מוחל לכל מי שהכעיס והקניט אותי או שחטא
כנגרי בין בגופי בין בממוני. בין בכבודי. בין בכל אשר לי בין באונס
בין ברצון בין בשוגג בין במזיד בין בדבור בין במעשה בין בגלגול זה.
בין בגלגול אחר. לכל בר ישראל ולא יענש שום אדם בסבתי יהי רצון
מלפניך יהוה אלהי ואלהי אבותי שלא אחטא עוד ולא
אחזור בהם ולא אשוב עוד להכעיסך ולא אעשה הרע בעיניך ומה
שחטאתי מחוק ברחמיך הרבים ולא על ידי יסורים וחלים יהיו לרצון
אמרי פי והגיון לבי לפניך יהוה צורי וגואלי ׃

Master of the Universe - I forgive everyone who has angered and upset me, or sinned against me, whether they did this physically, materialistically or disrespectfully. Whether they did this by accident or intentionally, with horrible evil thoughts or without thinking, whether they said the words or with actions, whether in this life or in previous lives, i forgive them... and please GOD do not punish or hurt them, do not bring any illness or anything bad against them as i forgive them completely - please GOD.

The sign that you have successfully forgiven another person, is that when you think of them, you no longer have any hatred feelings. In fact you should have no feelings toward them at all. They mean nothing at all, not to you, not to your life or nor to your soul.

If you still feel some element of hatred or any emotions towards them, this is a sign that you have NOT disconnected from them and their evil ways, and THIS WILL HURT, POISON AND DESTROY YOUR LIFE AND SOUL. So say the prayer above and FORGIVE them in your mind, thoughts and soul, forget about them, don't even mention their name, and detach yourself from them and their ways completely.

In forgiving these deceitful draining people and troubled souls we are actually freeing our own soul from any connection from such heavy depressed and sad people.

The higher level of forgiveness is that you actually feel sorry for their soul with a  genuine compassion and pray for them that they will also find GOD and the loving spiritual pathway in this physical life.

By understanding and accepting that there is a DIVINE plan for each and everyone of us, then there is no reason or point to getting upset, annoyed or angry, these are bad emotions that belong to bad people.

Good people only have LOVE, compassion and forgiveness. Life teaches us to learn to FORGET, FORGIVE and MOVE ON to a better future of wholesome LOVE.

## 3. Understanding the Concept of True Love אמתי אהבה

Pure true love is spiritual energy; hence it is unconditional upon anything physical. True love is attained through the connection on a level of the soul to the SPIRIT world.

True Love is the creative life-giving energy that connects one's soul to Spirit world; this LOVE connection energizes our soul with the יניקה

49

מלמעלה spiritual life energy that enlivens our soul from the DIVINE source of all pure creative physical and spiritual energy.

## What is "True Love" אמתי אהבה

"True Love" is a life-giving source of energy of UNCONDITIONAL love; it is not given nor taken but it is a GIFT of energy that energizes a person's soul with life energy.

The spiritual law of love is that love has a power to CREATE energy. When a person energizes one's heart with emotions of LOVE one is given an inner spiritual Divine motivational energy to accomplish actions, tasks which makes life happen.

## "Giving & Taking" OR "Creating"

People who only believe in the physical world, have beliefs of limitations, and do not believe in the infinite power of creative energy of LOVE. Therefore they live a limited-life based on "Giving & Taking", wherefore they live selfishly, by amassing energy and money for themselves by taking as much as possible from others and not giving. This leaves everyone they connect with drained, blocked and unloved, like they suck out life energy from everyone they connect with.

The Spiritual Law of LOVE and the basis of all the creations in the entire Universe is that LOVE is CREATED energy. Every LOVE emotion of every second of every day creates an energy and vitality that energizes a person mind, body and within one's soul with an aliveness and happiness. Therefore a spiritually enlightened person knows the ONLY way to generate a life energy is by CREATING LOVE energy.

# Creating Love Energy

1. The first way to create LOVE energy is to connect to the Divine source of LOVE which is through LOVE of GOD.

2. Secondly, one can create LOVE energy by thinking of and connecting with good loving spiritual souls in the Spirit world. People you knew when they were alive, and through the bond of pure unconditional LOVE that exists eternally, connects our soul with their souls in the Spiritual world.

3. Thirdly, learning to appreciate and give thanks for all the wonderful things we have in life, makes a persons heart fill with LOVE energy out of gratitude for the gift and opportunities of life.

4. Lastly and most importantly use words and expressions like "I love life", "I Love the way everything turns out in life", "I love the gift of life" and of course to continual say to one's loving soulmate, family, parents, children "I love you". Keep repeating the most powerful words in the English language:- "I love you" "I love you" "I love you" "I love you" "I love you" "I love you".

# Chapter 8

## Power of Life

### Understanding That a "Life of Love" Brings Energy, Love and Healing

The pure Divine spiritual creative and life-giving energy of love that flows from the Divine Spiritual realms is channeled into this world through enlightened souls and through all loving people, this life-giving energy is radiated from the soul and acts to give life energy and enlighten people all over the world.

The enlightened loving compassionate and spiritually-minded person acts to channel and bring to the world a life-giving energy, through the constant connection to the spiritual world such souls bring to this physical world the energy for others to live.

Everything we have and everything we are is identified in our soul by the amount of sincere love we bring into this world, the loving energy we glow and radiate, in this life, from previous lives and in the future eternal spiritual world. This measure of love that we exude each moment of every day identifies the spiritual level of our soul. The more compassion and love the more energy within our soul, the more hatred, jealousy, sadness and anger the less energy within our soul.

### Love versus Hate; Life versus Death

### Choose Life & Love ... בחיים בחרת

It is impossible to have two emotions at the same time, one can either have emotions of Love or emotions of Hate, and one can either be happy or sad. It is impossible to be positive and negative at the same time, the spirit soul is naturally either positive or negative; this is the freewill choice of living life.

52

When a person is positive, happy and loving a person is connected to the Divine life creative energy of GOD, whereas when a person is negative, destructive hateful and depressed one has disconnected from the Divine source of life, and of course it is impossible to be connected to GOD and disconnected to GOD, hence a person is either positive or negative, loving or hateful, alive or dead, creative or destructive, selfless or selfish, optimistic or pessimistic, spiritual or materialistic.

It is impossible to be loving and hateful at the same time, as all emotions of love connect one to life, whereas all emotions of hate disconnect one from life, even the most hateful and destructive people when "making love" with their spouses become loving and connect with life energy.

This is the freewill challenge of life and the constant internal struggle in life to always be vigilant of one's moods and emotions, ensuring one is always positive, constructive, compassionate, kind and loving to make the freewill choice to continually think of emotions of love which create and bring life, refusing to be negatively influenced by bad people and always blocking any negative emotions of hate, sadness depression and self-destruction.

**Focus On Loving Thoughts**

Every moment we have emotions and thoughts of love, we are connecting ourselves to GOD - the Divine source of all LIFE, thereby giving our soul energy and sustenance.

For every emotion of hate, jealousy, envy and sadness, one is disconnecting one's soul from the DIVINE life energy, and hence bringing death, sadness, depression and self-destruction into one's life.

**The Strength and Power of Ones Soul is measured By the Flow of Love**

A person's soul is identified by the amount of energy flowing through it. The strongest and most powerful people in the world channel more

53

thought energy into their mind, soul and body, and they share this energy with other people by giving out an energy that energizes other people's lives, through their thoughts or power of speech.

The eternal Divine energy of life is love; therefore a strong and powerful soul allows more love energy to channel through it than a weaker soul. The more a person gives to others the more a person brings into one's life, like a flowing river of life energy. love energy is selfless and the ONLY way to bring more love into one's life is by giving out love energy to other people.

The amount of flowing love energy one has in one's life indicates the amount of creative life energy, the more flowing loving energy in one's life the greater the potential power within one's soul.

People, who feel their life stagnant blocked and frustratingly dull where nothing new is happening in their life, feel this because there is no new loving life energy flowing into their lives. They are living from loving energy created in the past instead of creating new love energy in the present. Unblocking one's life must starts by allowing a new flow of love energy into one's life immediately NOW - in the present moment.

Start immediately by saying "GOD - I love you and thank you GOD for the gift of life", say "I love life" and of course "I love you" to one's soulmate, parents, children and family, pets and friends!

**Make the world a better place, light a candle for Love and say a prayer for other people to find love.**

Learn to show love and compassion by praying sincerely for other people, stop worrying about one's own life and start praying sincerely for other people with compassion, pity and love. Light a candle and say a prayer for them.

The more one prays with love for other people, the more one becomes a spiritual channel of love, a channeling source of life energy from spirit world to this physical world to help other people. Then the channel of life energy through one's soul will grow, radiating a loving energy that is magnetic for true happiness and love, in one's life and in everyone's life, making this world a better place to live.

Once a person has connected and feels the Divine life-giving energy of love flowing through one's soul, it is impossible to go back to a depressing life, and a new pathway of spiritual enlightenment is found.

# Radiating Love - Heals

Once a person learns to transform one's objectives from a life of selfish materialism into one of selfless spiritualism, then a person will be acting as a channel of life energy of love and compassion from the Divine spiritual realms. The person's soul will radiate and glow with an aura of life and love, everyone who connects, sees and senses such a person will be radiated by the spiritual glow of their soul.

This glowing spiritual energy of pure life energy is channeled by this soul, and acts to provide everyone, (even the non believers, who connect with such a good soul), with a source of life energy.

The Divine life energy of love creates life, sustains life and heals life, such a connection with a channel of spiritual life energy gives a persons soul the confidence, faith and inner power to live life to their fullest potential.

The transformation and opportunity for change will come in everyone's life after too many experiences when one feels continually drained, tired and depressed. Realizing that only thoughts of love and connections with channels of life energy to good souls, are instantaneously energizing one's life, then suddenly, like an internal light being switched-on, one learns, realizes and decides to change one's futile draining pathway and become a spiritual channel in the selfless service of GOD and learning to have faith in a "Life of Trust in GOD".

## Understanding The Eternal Spiritual Law Of Love; Love Can Never Be Destroyed.

The Divine source of energy for every single soul, everything in this physical universe and in the Divine Spirit world is the eternal Divine love, which can never be destroyed. No one or nothing can ever destroy this true love energy - this is the eternal spiritual law of love.

### "Created by GOD"

Everything created by GOD exists eternally; everything created in this physical Universe exists for eternity. Everything has been created with eternal Divine love. When we emulate our CREATOR and create with love this infuses a Divine life energy into that physical entity, hence children are conceived through love of the parents; plants, flowers and animals continue the cycle of life through love energy.

### "Created by GOD - Destroyed By Man"

Everything created by GOD exists for eternity, but it can be destroyed in this physical world by the evil of man.

The nature of mankind is to destroy. Every day our physical bodies eat wholesome food, fruit and vegetables turning this good food into disgusting poisonous smelly faeces-excrement. Every day our bodies convert good food into excrement, the more physical and greedier a person is, the more a person eats hence the more destruction a person is causing by creating more faeces-excrement.

Our challenge in life is to be more like the Divine creator of the Universe and create life energy more than we destroy. This is especially true in our generation, with the concern that we are destroying the air quality and protective ozone layer of the earth in the environment with every journey we make in gas-guzzling cars, causing damage to this planet earth and causing destructive climate change.

## The Less Influence of Man - The More Divine

The more mankind messes with creations of GOD, the more destruction caused, hence the most "natural" places on earth that have been created from the beginning of time at the creation of this Universe by GOD that are the most unspoilt by man have the most Divine energy.

This is the reason why everyone feels and appreciates the natural Divine energy of mountains, hills, green countryside, natural waterfalls, the seas, beaches and the sky. The less mankind's' destructive influence the more inherent GODLY energy infused within and upon it.

## Changing & Undoing the Past Destruction

יפה שעה אחת של אהבה יותר מאלף שנים של שנאה

"One moment of love gives more life and is worth more than a 1000 years of hate"

The foundational essence of ספר שינוים - Sefer Shinuyim, the Book of Changes, is that through one thought of LOVE, connecting one's soul to the Divine source of spiritual energy of LOVE one can change and have power more than 1000 years of hate and destruction.

Each and every thought we have creates energy, a loving thought has the power of GODLY eternal life energy, whereas a destructive thought only has the power of that moment, hence one focused thought of love can eradicate 1000's of years of hate energy.

## Hate Always Dies

When we think in hindsight of the history of the world, looking and laughing at the destruction of all the hateful, murderous and deadly empires such as the Egyptian, the Babylonians, the Greeks, the Romans, even the Turkish and Nazi German Empires, we see that NONE of these empires exist today. Remember the funny rhyme we used to say in school, at the useless learning of Latin, "Latin is a language as dead as can be - first it killed the Romans - now its killing me"!

All the hateful destructive regimes and enemies of good spiritually loving people כלל ישראל are all as dead, buried, forgotten and insignificant; the spiritually enlightened with its foundation and principles of LOVE and COMPASSION survives and outlives all hateful regimes. Hate always dies, love always survives lives eternally.

## The Eternal Divine GOD is LOVE

The essence and source of all goodness in the world is love. The power and energy of love eliminates all negativity, blockages, death, sadness and evil. The power and energy of love creates and brings down spiritual energy from eternal Divine Spiritual world which heals our souls and bodies in this physical world. Love is the key to everything in this world and journey we call "Life".

# Chapter 9
## The Wisdom of Astrology

Astrology is the study of the physical stars and planets in our solar system, their energies and effects on the individual person and collective universe.

The whole of the universe is continually moving in space according to a Divine plan of precise and exact motion. The enormity, vastness and magnitude of our solar system, the universe and stars is beyond our physical comprehension of human imagination. This is referred to as "EIN SOF" - אין סוף - infinity.

The planetary movements in our solar system and the stars visible to our eyes in the sky at night have spiritual laws and energies. Each and every planet has energies and strengths which are coordinated to affect everyone and everything on this planet Earth, in accordance to a Divine plan of time.

### Introduction

Our soul receives energy to live every second of every day from GOD. Our spiritual soul is connected to the spirit world, and receives its vitality through the transcending levels of energies from the spirit world. The closer we are and more connected we are spiritually - the greater our vitality and creative life energy. The creative life energy of this world is GOD, and GOD is LOVE, LOVE creates life, LOVE sustains life, and the lack of love or hate means death.

Our soul constantly receives energy from GOD and the eternal Divine spirit world, which is the spiritual sustenance our soul needs. Similarly our physical body also receives energies which give our lives the variety and change we need for our journey of life on earth. The study of the energy our physical body receives from the planets and stars is called Astrology.

The life giving energy from GOD and Spirit world is called "Yeneeka" - יניקה מלמעלה - "pure nourishment from heavens above".

"Yeneeka" is the name also given to breast-feeding, as "Yeneeka" is sustenance that is created from thoughts of love and a desire to provide energy to the soul through the energy of love, hence someone who does not know how to love or has no loving energy is as good as dead, as they are blocking the flow of life-energy to their body & soul.

The secret of Jewish astrology is to be aware that we have a soul, and that the energy of GOD can override and supercedes everything, through the love we have for GOD and for the love given to us by GOD, we will always receive energy to live, if only we are open and loving to receive the "Yeneeka" from GOD, through the astrological energy of the planets.

The awareness that we have a soul in our physical body is of vital importance to understanding Jewish astrology, and will enable one to understand concepts of Astrology perfectly with pure truthfulness.

In this chapter we shall teach the following basic Jewish spiritual astrological concepts:-

1.  The concept of "Yeneeka", the importance to the place of birth and where one lives.
2.  The concept of one's real astrological birthday is "the day of conception", the day one's soul and one's physical journey started on earth, and of course one's real birthday when one became detached from one's mother at birth.
3.  Understanding the 12 signs of the zodiac, the purpose of variety in mankind. Understanding the 4 groups of signs; water, earth, fire and air, the collective purpose of each group and reasons why instantaneously some people connect and others don't connect.
4.  The concept of cycle of life, the 12 periods of 7 years of life, making a full life of 84 years. The concept of living the 12 periods of life in one year. The yearly cycle of life and the lessons of each month of the year.

# 1. The Concept of YENEEKA

## The Importance to the Place of Birth and Where one Lives.

In the same way we eat and drink, giving our body energy to live and survive. Our soul needs spiritual energy to survive.

יניקה מלמעלה - Yeneeka Milmaala - is the place where one receives one's energy from spirit world. It is a specific place in this physical world. This is the physical place where you should be living, and is the place your soul is yearning and searching for your physical body to move to.

If you are not living or were not born in that place, then you will find that you need to sleep more than most people, so that your soul can travel to that place whilst you sleep and feel recharged and energized. These signs should identify to you that you must MOVE from where you are living. Astrology will teach you to identify where the energy is best for one to live.

However, before you contemplate moving, you need to ask yourself honestly, why have you been born and put in the situation you are in. Is it because you have made mistakes in your life and got side-tracked or have you had no choice, and this is where your life has placed you. In either case, now that you are aware of knowledge from your enlightened spiritual learning. It is now time to change; your soul is now awakened and ready to make the changes.

## The Place of Birth

In the spiritual concept of "Yeneeka", it is vitally imperative that you consider the place of your birth and if you can - find out the place of your conception, if it's different, this indicates that your soul started its journey in one place, with the energy of that place and then collected the energy of everywhere your mother traveled until your birth. For this reason Jewish mothers are careful where they go during pregnancy so as not to disturb nor damage the spiritual soul of the child they are carrying.

61

In considering the place of birth, one should learn about and understand the energy that town/city is famous for and at the time of your conception and birth.

For example, Liverpool UK, became worldwide famous in 1963 when the Beatles revolutionized the music world. The creative loving transformation they made catalyzed a whole generation to change. The Beatles and the energy of Liverpool identifies with rebelling against the past, encouraging freedom of expression life through love. Anyone born or conceived in Liverpool in 1963 and 1964 has the potential energy to catalyze a change the world like the Beatles did for the music world, culture and society.

Other examples of places of birth, with specific energies that are associated with it; New York, considered be many to be the number 1 city of the world, with the tallest of sky scrapers on Manhattan, and a concentrated centre of capitalist business and materialism in the whole world; Paris - city of love and romance; Rome - thoughts of the Roman Empire and of religion of Christianity.

Similarly, places can have meanings in peoples mind as places of death, tragedy, bad luck. Once labeled by our minds and thoughts, people born and associated with that place carry this negative energy. For example, Beslan Russia, Chernobyl, Izmit Turkey (the 30,000 dead in earthquake in 1999), Bam Iran (earthquake of Dec 26th 2003), Sri Lanka, Nicobar and all the places affected by Tsunami tidal wave of Dec 26th 2004 etc.,

Learn about the PLACE of your conception and birth. Learn about the history and events that occurred in the world at the time of your conception and birth.

Learn about the history of the place you are currently living in, what energies are associated with this place? What lessons do you need to learn in living there? What type of energy is your soul receiving? Is it life-giving good and creatively constructive or draining and deadly destructive?

After understanding the different energies of places in the world, some blessed and being given the gift of life and love, whilst other places are a focus of negative destructive emotions of hatred, violence and death. Then ask and pray for spiritual guidance to be guided to live in the right place for your soul.

## 2. Ones Spiritual Astrological Birthday

Spiritual Astrology teaches that one's physical creation is the day of conception, the day one's soul and one's physical journey started on earth. Spiritual and physical events happen concurrently in synchronous and harmonious conjunction with each other. So the time you where conceived is the time your physical journey starts.

### Conception and Birth

Jewish spiritual astrology is based on the fact that the precise moment one is conceived is the astrological identity of one's soul, as this is the moment that the soul that transcends from the Spirit world, the astrological energies of the planets at conception truly identifies the energy of one's soul and physical life on earth. This major difference is the reason why some astrologers are not able to forecast the future, as they are using the natal birthday.

The book Raziel Hamalach, רזיאל המלאך, states clearly that the astrological time of your arrival on this planet, is the moment your physical journey starts. That is the moment of conception, of course this is almost impossible to know, unless your parents are extremely sensitive and spiritually aware to have known this moment, when they felt your soul arrive in their bodies.

Nonetheless one should consider the Sun sign aspects of your approximate date on your conception. This will help you identify your character, known as the "Yesod" - יסוד – "Foundation" Sun sign of your astrological identity.

For example, everyone assumes Librans, whom are born in September - October, are loving, flexible, easily changeable moods, and have many friends. Yet they are also known to be very stubborn, determined, resist changes and have very few really close friends they can talk to completely honestly . That is because most Librans are in essence, conceived in 9 months prior in December - January, and during the Sun sign of Capricorn, are ruled by restrictive, slow and gracefully moving Saturn.

And for another example, a person born in Sun sign of Pisces, is actually conceived in Gemini, the quality of dual personality of a person conceived in Gemini is reflected in Pisces born person, as the constant fight between right and wrong, good and bad, spiritual and selfish materialism etc., Once this person has transformed their character - they can become into a selfless spiritual kindhearted Pisces natured person. This is the purpose of their journey of life on earth.

So check out your astrology for nine months before you were born at approximate moment of conception. Have you ever felt that something new always comes in your life three months after your birthday? That is indeed because astrologically it is the birthday of your physical journey in this world - the conception.

Ones astrological character is identified by the date of one's conception "birthday", this is your intrinsic character instilled and infused within your soul.

Your natal birthday character is the character that you as an individual - without any parental and social influences will change into if you are 100% detached from your parents and social circumstances. In many cases, it is the character you are continually striving to become and change-into during your life.

The qualities of the character of natal birthday, is your potential result once you have transformed and developed your character, fulfilling your purpose in life. We all have come to earth to change and transform. This is the Sun sign given to you to identify your pathway of change during this life.

It is well known that when children grow up and leave home, developing their own independence and character - they can be remarkably changed from their childhood character. This is the character of "detachment" from one's mother - the natal birth character. If one has not yet transformed into the character, then usually at the moment when parents die, especially if one was attached to one's mother, this suddenly catalyses changes in the person's character. This new and destined character is the natal birth character.

## 3. Understanding the 12 Signs of the Zodiac

**The 12 Star Signs**

| Aries | 21st March - 20th April |
|---|---|
| Taurus | 20th April - 21st May |
| Gemini | 21st May- 21st June |
| Cancer | 21st June - 22nd July |
| Leo | 22nd July - 23rd August |
| Virgo | 23rd August - 23rd September |
| Libra | 23rd September - 22nd October |
| Scorpio | 23rd October - 22nd November |
| Sagittarius | 22nd November - 22nd December |
| Capricorn | 22nd December - 20th January |
| Aquarius | 20th January - 21st February |
| Pisces | 22nd February - 21st March |

The purpose of variety in mankind is to make each individual humble and aware that one is just "one piece in a whole picture", no-one is perfect nor contains the characteristics of everything and everyone. We are all individual pieces that come together to perform our personal and collective purpose in life. The variety in life gives each individual uniqueness as well as an awareness and quality of belonging to the "soul group of the collective world". The 4 groups of

Sun signs are categorized by the 4 elements; water, earth, fire and air.

## The Four Elements

| FIRE | Aries, Leo, Sagittarius. |
|------|--------------------------|
| EARTH | Taurus, Virgo, Capricorn. |
| AIR | Gemini, Libra, Aquarius |
| WATER | Cancer, Scorpio, Pisces |

Reb Chaim Vital, the famous Jewish kabbalist who wrote the "Book of Reincarnations" Sefer Gilgulim. Explains the four elements of nature, each of which come with its own specific mission and test in life to overcome:-

The FIRE signs have a tendency to be exceedingly selfish and proud; their lesson in life is therefore to become more considerate of others, kind and selfless. Also to become more humble in their behavior by learning consideration for other people feelings and emotions. The Fire sign can be overbearing intimidating and "burn" people, the fire sign needs to learn to control its temperament, to control and provide the right amount of energy when it is needed, and not to be so overbearing that pushes people away.

The EARTH signs have a tendency to be lazy and depressed their lesson in life is to create activity and keep themselves busy. Additionally even when they are busy they must make sure they have the right attitude, thinking positive constructive thoughts, avoiding depressive, sad, negative or jealous thoughts. Once the earth sign learns to control its energy it can provide very solid foundations for any project or venture.

The AIR signs have a tendency to talk too much and to tell lies, sometimes with their sharp tongues they can hurt and damage other people. They must learn to tell the truth and communicate positive loving thoughts with other people, giving people constructive encouragement and support with their words. Learning to control the power of speech and communication can help to join together all facets of society.

The WATER signs have a tendency to follow their animal instincts, instead of thinking of the difference between right and wrong. They have a tendency for too much and excessiveness in eating, drinking and sex. Therefore, they must learn to control themselves and their animal instincts. Once controlled, they provide necessary sustenance to provide life to the world.

**Why do you connect wonderfully with some people, horribly with others, and some people you don't connect with at all?**

In astrological terms you are looking for someone on your level, with a vibration of their physical and spiritual soul in harmony with yours. This is based on the 4 elements of nature. As each astrological sign vibrates to one of 4 basic groups:-

| FIRE | Aries, Leo, Sagittarius. |
| EARTH | Taurus, Virgo, Capricorn. |
| AIR | Gemini, Libra, Aquarius |
| WATER | Cancer, Scorpio, Pisces |

For example in the same logical way "Fire" is extinguished by "Water", so too in astrological spiritual terms, the "fire sign" person will feel extinguished by the "water sign". Looking at each combination of each the groups:-

**Fire signs**

**ARIES, LEO and SAGITTARIUS** are the Fire signs. Though they sparkle in different ways, they are all passionate, and restless. Don't look here for a quiet life. Be ready for a temper that flares up at the slightest provocation but then rapidly burns out. Be ready too, to face irrepressible ambition. Fire fancies itself as invincible. Though it is always hungry and in a hurry, it thinks that sooner or later, it can wear down the most resistant material and make it come ablaze. If a Fire sign person wants you as a partner, you'll find it hard to damp down their enthusiasm. Saying no will merely make you seem like more of a challenge. If you really don't want the heat, keep well away from the kitchen. But some like it hot... and those who do are right in their element here.

## Air signs

**GEMINI, LIBRA and AQUARIUS** are the Air signs who dwell in the realm of thought and theory. Their heads are always in the clouds. From this lofty position they can see a long way and find a lot to say. If you enjoy conversation, debate and discussion, here's your perfect partner. Not so if you happen to feel there's more to life than words. An Air sign person can say pretty much anything and make it sound persuasive. So persuasive, indeed, that they will convince themselves it must be true! Woes betide you if you argue. That's playing right into the Air person's hands. Air likes to whip up a wind. It also likes to be free to float. If you like things to be the same from day to day, Air's constant changeability will drive you bananas. If though, you like to get high on the exhilarating oxygen of brainpower, here's your source of eternal excitement.

## Earth signs

**TAURUS, VIRGO and CAPRICORN** are the Earth signs. They are solid and strong. Or so, at least, they seem. Think though, of soil and the way it surges with invisible, life-giving energy. Or consider a tree. Though very much 'of the earth' it is constantly in a state of change. It adapts to the seasons and never stops growing. Earth sign people, despite their image of implacability, are sensitive, sensual and subject to slow but steady change. They possess enormous power and love to put this to a fruitful use. The further into the earth you dig, the more hidden treasure you find. If you seek depth and meaning, an Earth sign person is your ideal companion and likewise, if you want loyalty, dedication and integrity. If though, you thrive on drama, adventure or debate, you may prefer someone with whom the ground rules are less clearly defined.

## Water signs

**CANCER, SCORPIO, and PISCES** are the intuitive and emotional Water signs. They wear their hearts on their sleeves and rightly so, for their hearts are pure and kind. Though they pretend, in different ways, to be dry, they can't help but well up with compassion at the slightest sob story. But they can afford to be a little more giving than the rest of us because, for all their apparent insecurity, they can never come to real harm. It's easy to disperse water but hard to destroy it. Sooner or later, even if it has to seep underground or evaporate in order to escape, water always finds its way to more water. If you seek a companion full of heartfelt feeling, look no further. If you prefer less fluidity or you fear being swamped by ever-changing moods, you're out of your depth here.

**The combination of the groups relate to each other as follows:-**

**Fire and Fire**

Fire is always attracted to more fire. The question, when you put two fire people together, is not 'will they be drawn to one another' but 'will the relationship burn itself out?' It certainly will if there's too much competition for the same source of fuel. How then, can you prevent a Fire sign partnership from flaring up wildly, only to go out in a blaze of glory? You need a totally shared sense of purpose. You have to turn your fire on a common enemy, not on each other or reach an agreement about what you are trying to achieve together. Even with such a deal struck, sparks will occasionally fly. Fire people love a challenge. They can't resist infuriating each other every so often. Then again, if you thrive on passion, there are some distinct advantages to life with someone who can always get you feeling fully inflamed.

**Fire and Earth**

Earth is covered in vegetation which fire can burn. Deep below the earth there's coal and oil, even more substantial fuel for fire. It is easy then, to see why Fire people are drawn to Earth people. They provide constant psychological fuel for the fiery person to consume. Why though, should an Earth person fancy a Fire person? Where's the advantage in getting together with someone who will take all you've got to give and come back for more? The Earth person is understandably cautious. But the Earth person does have a need for fire. You can see this more clearly if you appreciate how sensuous Earth types truly are. They yearn to feel the earth move and nothing makes the earth move more dramatically than an explosion! That's why, if this relationship gets off the ground, it turns out to be such dynamite.

**Earth and Air**

Without earth's gravity, there would be no air. Without air, earth would be incapable of supporting life. People born under these two elements are strongly drawn to one another. Air people benefit greatly from having a partner who will ground them. Earth people (who need stimulation if they are ever to get anywhere) enjoy the flow of ideas that only an air person can offer. In theory then, this is a perfect union. In practice, there are a few little problems. Tornados, for example, blow up when the Air person can find no other way to make the Earth person shift. Or underground caverns that entice in fresh air and then, by sealing up their entrances with a sudden rock fall, trap it there forever. These risks though, can be avoided. And, when they are, no relationship can match it ... in heaven or on earth!

**Earth and Water**

To understand this relationship, consider the contrast between land and sea. Imagine these forces in perpetual battle; think of mighty waves, crashing against rocks, earth and water themselves seem to enjoy unleashing all that energy. Earth and Water people have a similar tendency to clash superficially but form a deep, fulfilling, lasting bond. They are not always instantly drawn together but slowly, they find a way to coexist. The more they do, the more they see how much they can offer each other. Soil needs rain in order to be fertile. Rivers need banks if they are to stay on track. Earth and Water people need each other for inspiration and support. Only when they fail to keep separate identities and try to 'merge' do we get a problem. Water mixed with Earth makes mud ... but then, some of us feel that even this is glorious!

**Earth and Earth**

What happens when irresistible force meets immovable object? Put two Earth sign people together and you'll find out! In theory, there's potential for endless pressure; a battle for ultimate supremacy between two tectonic plates that can only ever end in an earthquake. In fact, it rarely comes to this. Earth sign people are never drawn to each other unless they can both sense a viable way to share the territory. Agreement from the outset, is imperative. But lively relationships need just a small amount of friction. If you dare not allow even the tiniest amount of this to develop for fear of starting something that you can never finish, the result is likely to be a partnership that trundles, uneventfully on and on... and on...

## Water and Water

What does water want, more than anything else? To find its way to yet more water! Think how inland streams make their way across the country till they reach first the river then the ocean. Water people have a similar, natural desire to seek one another's company. There they find a level of empathy that nobody else can match. Even Water sign people who happily marry individuals of another element, will ensure they keep a fair selection of Water friends. Not all Water relationships though, are an instant success. Warm water tends to float, in a slightly superior way, over cold. Fresh water will try to keep itself from salt water. Some waters merge more naturally than others and all have a difficult time when it comes to separating. Every water/water marriage is 'for life', no matter how often or how intensely both may try to part.

## Air and Air

"Who can see the wind? Neither you nor I, but when the tree bows down its head, the wind is rushing by. What are we to conclude though when we see that tree nodding wildly up and down like a teenage heavy metal fan? Surely this can only mean that it is being blown by two winds at once. Air sign people have no difficulty forming a rapport with one another - kindred spirits who feel, from the moment they meet, that they are renewing an old acquaintance. When they're in agreement, they're closer than a pair of lovebirds. When they're not, they're like clowns back to back on a tandem, each trying to pedal in the opposite direction. It's then that the relationship stops being a breeze and turns, instead, into a wild hurricane. Air sign people never agree to differ. They like contradicting each other too much.

71

## Air and Water

Put air into water and you get lovely bubbles. Put water into air and you get soft, fluffy clouds - provided that there's not too much pressure. We all know though, what happens to a fizzy drink if it's shaken. We also know how atmospheric pressure can cause water in the atmosphere to turn into something very cold and clammy. Air and water go well together... most of the time. Air sign people provide intuitive Water people with much-needed intellectual perspective. Water people return the compliment by compensating for the Air person's dry attitude. But while they can visit one another's domain, they cannot remain in it for long. The bubbles go flat after a while. Likewise, the clouds tend to disperse. This relationship has to be constantly renewed and revived. It is though, well worth the maintenance.

## Fire and Water

Put fire under water and you get steam. Place water over fire and you put the fire out. Everything depends, in this relationship, on who takes the lead. Hot water is more powerful than cold. When water is changed by fire, it makes greater impact. No wonder then, that Water people find Fire folk appealing. They have nothing to fear. They know they can quench fire if it gets too hot. But why should a Fire person want to get close to a natural force that can destroy it? There is no logical answer. Water has nothing to offer Fire, but it needs it and wants it. That's why it works so hard to attract it! Fire is willing to be drawn because it hungers to be powerful in any way it can. It can't resist that steamy sizzle. Fire likes living dangerously. Water likes to get excited. This pairing may not be wise but it's hard for either to resist.

## Fire and Air

Fire needs air. Without it, no matter how much fuel it has, it cannot survive. Why though, does air need fire? It can exist quite nicely without all that smoke. It's the heat that it seeks. As any meteorologist will tell you, air currents are driven by temperature changes. Wind will not develop and travel unless something warms it up. Air sign people then, find Fire sign folk useful. They get them to stop sitting around thinking and they make them start doing things. There is strong attraction between these elements but there's also an ever-present danger. Fire folk glow so brightly in an Air person's company that they forget to refuel. Then, the wind ends up putting out the fading fire. But as long as there's even a tiny spark remaining, a breeze can rekindle it. Thus this relationship can carry on blowing hot and cold for a lifetime.

# 4. The Cycle of Life

### Life consists of 12 periods of 7 years

According to traditional Jewish astrology, a person's life is split up into 12 sections of 7 years making a total lifespan of 84 years.

The first 7 years one is like an ARIES ram, always putting oneself first selfishly and running around causing mayhem in complete irregular fashion, just like a newborn ram.

The next 7 years from 7 till 14, one is like a TAURUS bull, full of energy and fighting for one's space.

From 14 until 21 one transforms and becomes like twins GEMINI, developing a split personality from a child to an adult, with opinions and attitudes like a child and that of an adult.

From 21 till 28 like the sign CANCER, with changeable moods as one is sampling and tasting everything in early adulthood and adapting to changeable views of life, in the same way that Cancer is ruled by the ever changing Moon.

From 28 till 35 one becomes to one's physical peak and strength of the LEO lion, which identifies one's character, and usually the unchangeable course one has taken in life.

From 35 till 42 one settles into a semi permanent, yet orderly, well organized earth state of the intelligent young VIRGO.

From 42 till 49, one becomes the intelligent, thoughtful and communicative LIBRAN, balancing out and harmonizing life, with experience and ability to communicate one's thoughts sensibly.

From 49 till 56 like the Scorpio, a person develops an intense personality with hidden depths. SCORPIO has learnt through life experiences and no longer has fears. It can handle most situations.

From 56 till 63 like a Sagittarian full of optimism and encouragement, from life it has learnt and matured, nurtured its one character and able to reflect back on life positively with an exuding confidence developed and earned from experience. Therefore one is able to convincingly instill optimism.

From 63 till 70 like a Capricorn, they start to become introverted and take a very contemplative look at life. This can lead to depression and taking a damp look at life, they start to take a rigid and emotionally cold outlook on life. This stage in life they become very disciplined and fixed in their ways with little flexibility, which can be a good attribute if they have developed a fine character in their life, or a really depressing nuisance if they have failed.

From 70 till 77 like a unpredictable and communicative AQUARIAN, they have extremely fixed opinions, but are prepared to share their views with others, and start to talk and communicate their ideas and thoughts, even if only by reminiscing.

From 77 till 84 like a spiritual deep-thinking PISCES, idealistic sensitive and intuitive, no longer thinking about the everyday worries they had when younger, they are learning to look at and appreciate the deeper more emotional meaning of life . Becoming selfless and giving to others in an inspirationally spiritual way, using all their years of experience from their whole life and using these years to reflect on the true good memories and sensory pleasures of life, like music, nature and art.

In some circumstances, especially in the case of reincarnated souls, a young person may have developed their soul in previous lifetime and choose to continue where they left this world, hence a 40 year old may already be advising and thinking like a wise spiritual 80 year old !

## The Yearly Cycle of Life - Each Year Contains 12 Months

Each person has a yearly life cycle, whereby one's soul experiences the same type of lessons each and every year at the same time of year, as their soul is influenced by the movement of the sun in that sun sign. This yearly cycle is known as the movement through the 12 astrological HOUSES. Each month has its own specific energy, purpose and lessons to learn. The purpose of understanding each months energy is in order to learn to flow with lifes energy instead of fighting the destiny of life !

Remember - Jewish astrology teaches the first month is from the month of conception !

This is an important fact when understanding the energy of each month, the remaining 12 houses will only make perfect sense if one calculates the start from day/month of conception . As we explained above, the 30 days before one's "conception birthday" is the 12th house - one's spiritual house, this period is one's most intuitive and spiritual, as spiritual knowledge and energy flows into one's soul at this time.

The concept of each of the 12 months of the year as a reflection in part of the 12 periods in one's whole life cycle is also relevant, but the HOUSES have a more refined energy for each particular month.

## The Twelve Houses – Months of Each and Every Year

Each house represents each month of YOUR year, the 1st house starts with the 1st month from the month you were conceived. eg if you are born on 9th September you were conceived say 9th December, then 1st house of SELF is from 9th December till 9th January etc., each and every year the cycle of monthly energies pertain to that month for you.

## First House

This is the field of experience in which you are challenged to develop your own unique identity and present it to the world. Traditionally this house is associated with personal appearance.

## Second House

This is the field of experience in which you are challenged to define and refine your personal sense of values. The things, talents, and qualities that you treasure, cherish, enjoy, and hold on to for security is here, personal possessions and material wealth. Traditionally this house is associated with; inner and outer talents and resources, personal values.

## Third House

This is the field of experience in which you are challenged to organize personal experiences to form your own unique picture of the world, and then communicate your perceptions to others. Traditionally this house is associated with; brothers and sisters; basic education; eye-hand coordination and manual dexterity.

## Fourth House

This is the field of experience in which you are challenged to develop your capacity for emotional closeness; to find a feeling of security; and to face the effects your early childhood experiences had upon you. Traditionally this house is associated with; nurturing; inherited traits; unconditional love; the type of home you establish.

## Fifth House

This is the field of experience in which you are challenged to develop your creativity and self-esteem, and to find joy in living. Traditionally this house is associated with; children; enthusiasm; creativity; and motivation.

## Sixth House

This is the field of experience in which you are challenged to seek competence; to function efficiently, in your physical body and in your work. Traditionally this house is associated with; work; health; services; habit patterns; food; diet; pets.

## Seventh House

This is the field of experience in which you are challenged to develop committed relationships with others. Traditionally this house is associated with; your attitudes toward spouses and partners; intimate relationships; marriage; friends; dealings with the public; what you look for in others.

## Eighth House

This is the field of experience in which you are challenged to boldly wrest all the powers of your psyche from the deep, dark underworld; focus all that power with ruthless intensity on the process of breaking down your reality structure into little pieces, then reassemble all the pieces into a new whole. Here is the place where all the taboos of society are addressed; where you dig into your own "internal garbage" to find the treasure hidden there. Think of a compost heap where all the bits of decaying food break down and eventually turn into fertilizer to nourish new growth. Traditionally this house is associated with; other people's resources (possessions, money); sex; death and regeneration.

## Ninth House

This is the field of experience in which you are challenged to broaden your philosophical perspectives and to realize your highest potentials. Traditionally this house is associated with; the higher mind; higher education; law; in-laws; grand children.

## Tenth House

This is the field of experience in which you are challenged to earn respect and recognition in the world. Traditionally this house is associated with; ambition; status; reputation; career; the parent who set limits for you as a child.

## Eleventh House

This is the field of experience in which you are challenged to establish a relationship with group consciousness and contribute your gifts to community. Traditionally this house is associated with; humanitarian organizations; associations; friends; hopes, wishes and ambitions; shared ideals.

## Twelfth House

This is the field of experience in which you are challenged to explore your inner depths in solitude and silence; to discern between illumination and illusion, between spiritual growth and escapism. Before you can transcend the definitions of reality that confine you, you must be willing to let go of them. These definitions often have to become uncomfortable before we want to let go of them. Disillusionment and the experience of "bad luck" can create the desire to move through and beyond what is causing the pain. This is the house where spiritual knowledge and intuitive thoughts, plans and ideas flow easily into one's mind; it also tries to create situations if one has been side-tracked from a spiritual pathway to a materialistic pathway. This is certainly the month one should be focused SPIRITUALLY and not materially!

For those people whom have studied astrology and wondered why certain astrology aspects never fitted-in with reality, this is because the person was looking at the pattern of houses from BIRTH and not conception. When one looks carefully at each house for each month, then "astrology" starts to make sense! Planning the months of the year in accordance with spiritual astrology, helps a person go with the natural spiritual flow of life and destiny.

## Much More to Learn About Astrology

There is much to Jewish Spiritual Astrology than we have explained, such as is taught in the books "Sefer Raziel", on our website www.raziel.info , including such features as the "monthly astrological events", and for weekly horoscopes see my wife's website www.whatmazal.com.

# Chapter 10

## The Ancient Wisdom of PALMISTRY

Palmistry is the study of the lines of the palms of the hands. This section is taken from the ancient handwritten book of Sefer חכמת יד "Chochmas Yad"-"Wisdom & Knowledge of Palmistry", and explains three aspects to Palmistry and "the hands" :-

1.  The lines on the hand represent the pathway and "blue-print" of one's life "destiny", the pre-arranged plan and one's life journey is mapped out and indicated to an exact plan, as indicated by the precision of the lines on everyone's hand.

2.  The ancient art of Palmistry teaches that each person is unique. When one understands that the strength and individuality of one's' soul is contained within the precision of each of the lines of one's hands, this opens up a door in one's mind and soul to the importance of recognizing this perfect precision of Palmistry that GOD has created our physical body with a perfect exactness and is a reflection of our soul, so that each and every line our hands are perfectly accurate.

3.  Understanding that the hands are the most powerful connection between one's physical existence and one's spiritual soul, everyone's hands hold the key to one's spirituality. Using the power contained within one's hands and soul brings healing, positive energy, inner spiritual and physical strengthening. Leading to an understanding of the true power of praying with one's hands, shaking hands, holding hands, saluting, clapping, and using one's hands to protect one's souls and keep one's soul and aura clean.

## 1. The lines on one's hand indicate destined pathway of one's life.

### The difference between right and left hand

Most people will find the lines are similar but only slightly different on each hand. The lines on the left hand are the map of the journey that you were supposed to take when you were born. The lines on the right hand reflect the actual journey you have taken, they will be for the most part a reflection of the left, unless of course you have gone away from your destined path, or made considerable changes. Usually there is a small island on the life line symbolizing two potential pathways to the same end result, both are destined, neither is right or wrong .

### The hands represent one's personal destiny, identity and soul's journey

The purpose of studying palmistry is to give re-assurance to know that each person's life is unique and purposeful, even the several failed relationships, marriages / divorces, children, etc. Our hands have the blue-print of our individual life pathway stamped upon it . There are NO two hands in the whole world the same, as is known even "finger-prints" used by police world wide, are used to identify individuals.

### Reading the lines on the hand

# אורך ימים בימינה עושר וכבוד בשמאלה

This Hebrew sentence above is the Jewish prayer we say when we lift the Scroll of the Torah, with both hands, after reading it in the synagogue, and taken from book of proverbs chapter 3 verse 16, it means "Life is in the right hand, wealth and honour in the left hand".

According to Reb Chaim Vital, the right hand gives us the destiny of our life, and the variances in our left hand indicate the gain/loss of wealth, success and fame. Which correlates to the well known fact that "left -handed" people are more likely to be wealthy and famous.

For most readings it is easier to read the right hand, (and only for checking and clarity we look at the left - unless of course the person is left handed). From the hand below, you can see there are three main lines: - the life line, head line and heart line.

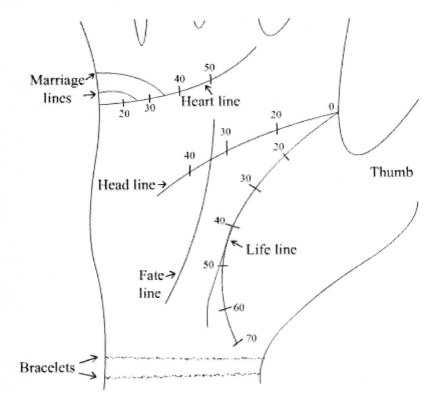

From the hand above, the numbers 20, 30, 40, 50 etc refer to age in years. These are approximate and vary on each persons hand according to the size of one's palm. Please read the sections below for explanations of each of the lines.

## The Life Line

The life line runs in a curve, it starts just above the thumb, between the thumb and the first finger, it runs downwards to the wrist. It indicates the course of one's life. A short life line does NOT mean a short life - but a short life line means that the significant purpose and intensity and strength of energy of your life to "set you up" for the whole of your life is in your younger years, once you are established with partner/children then you life has found its purpose and vitality.

## A Major Break in the Life Line

A break in the life line or an island simply means another opportunity to start over life anew on a different course. In our generation where many people are indeed reincarnated souls, we have come to earth to relive several past-lives, all of which are contained in this one life, hence we find that our lives have sections of COMPLETE changes, that brings changes in marriages and lifestyles, changes in circumstances of where we live, or even changes in religion and faith .

We consider this gift of being reincarnated a special blessing and gift. As we are so lucky to have many different parts to our "whole life" which means different objectives and sometimes different relationships for each major part of the life change, unless you have chosen to do this with your true soulmate.

## An Island in the Life Line

It is accepted that the point directly under the middle finger is your age 35, (mid life). From the photo (turn over to next page) of the hands of the famous man one can see an island in both hands, this island starts about age 30 and ends age 40 (approx) which indicates two alternative pathways to the same end result.

An island is simply an opportunity and choice in life to take two possible ways to the same end result. However, during the transition of going through an island, it is like "life" has gone on hold, for the period of the island, a detour has been taken, and when the period of the Island detour has been taken, coming back on track is like transforming and arriving back home after a long journey. From the hands below where there is destined island, when he arrived back at age 40 from the detour at age 30, it was as easy as coming back home after a holiday! Even though when he came back into the lives of the people they were indeed affected deeply when we left and when he returned.

**Forks at the End of the Life Line**

From the ages of 45 there is usually a fork, this simply offers two different alternatives, most 40 year olds experience some type of mid-life crisis where they have the potential to change and alter their life, in accordance to the foundation of aims, goals and objectives that they have worked on themselves from the age of 30, after the period known as the "Saturn return of 29-30", (see astrology chapter for explanation).

Both these diverging lifestyles are destined, potential and correct, but they are exceedingly different. One pathway simply continues the life one has have lived until then, another life pathway takes a divergence. Usually the diverting and different pathway has an extended life, much longer than the other continued life. This is indeed a sign to represent that if the person changes their lifestyle, choosing to be brave and live a life they really enjoy as opposed to the life they are stuck with, then they will be blessed with a longer and healthier life. A permanent fork on any line offers a choice of life, which is irreversible once the decision is taken.

**Inner Life Lines**

Inner lifelines, these are usually faint lines, shorter than the life line, sometimes they only accompany the life line for very short periods. They follow the same direction as the life line, and are located between the life line and the thumb; they are situated on the "Mound of the Thumb".

These inner lifelines are an indication that a person is blessed with spiritual guides and angels that are accompanying a person in their life. The purpose of spirit life energy, guides and helpers, is to help maximize and fulfill one's full potential. They are an extra source of spiritual help, life vitality and energy, in order to assist a person to fulfill their aims, ambitions and purpose in life; inner life lines indicate an extra added advantage to one's life.

## The Heart Line

The Heart line is immediately below the fingers; it starts beneath the little finger, known as the "pinky", and moves across the hand finishing beneath the middle or first finger. This line deals with one's love life.

## Lines going UP or DOWN from heart line

The lines going down from your heart line reflect the bad/hateful relationships you have to go through in life , the lines going up from the heart line are the good passionate loving relationships you are given in life .

## First Experience of Love

From the age of 15-20 on the heart line, there will be lines going up towards and joining themselves to the end of your hand beneath your little finger - these are potential "marriage" love lines. In soulful palmistry, marriage love lines do not necessarily mean that you will marry the person. One may choose just to live and make love with the potential marriage partner. Or have a "crush" on them, connecting one's thoughts and soul with their soul and thoughts.

The first experience of love has profound affects on a person, as it is the opening of a whole new world. In the innocence of first love, one's soul is strong and more idealistic in love. Looking for a wholesome soulful connection as opposed to sexual desires or selfish materialistic benefits of relationships, as one matures in the adult world. A person who is lucky to meet their soulmate in these younger idealistic years is considered blessed.

Nonetheless, if one feels one has "gone off" the correct and destined pathway in life, then one can think back to those "first love" years; this is one method to find a way to reconnect with the innocence of love and find one's true soulmate. Accordingly all psychologists such as Prof. Dr Carl Jung, explain the reason why people in "mid-life" try instinctively to revisit their childhood, is an attempt to reconnect with their true destiny and true love. Believing that the pathway they have taken is wrong; as they are experiencing that they have no true love or soul satisfaction in life, with a sense of "lacking someone" special.

## Marriage Lines

On everyone's hand, there are lines going upwards from the heart line, these are potential love marriage lines. There are also some lines going down from the heart line, these are negative influences or failed relationships that have turned hateful and troublesome.

Sometimes we meet our potential love, and the line is completed all the way to the side of the hand. Sometimes we miss the love of our life, or it is ruined - which is indicated by a break in the marriage line. There will always be at least two or three chances for LOVE in life - one may indeed meet those potential destined loves, if one is in a marriage or committed relationship, then the test is not to get involved or be a test for a person to make a decision !

## Marriage Lines are also known as "Commitment lines"

The lines going up from the heart line are traditionally known as "marriage" lines. However the truth is that for some people, a love of work or commitment to a project, life ambition, desires or most importantly an idealistic service of GOD, as with dedicated monks, nuns, priests and spiritual leaders.

This strong idealistic commitment is actually seen in palmistry as a marriage line. "Married" in the spiritual service to GOD. Of course they maybe tested like everyone else to prove their commitment in their devout relationship. As every "commitment" means the constant testing and reaffirming of one's commitment to that "one love" of one's life.

In much the same way, but in quite a sharp contrast to is, the very ambitious materialistic career people are so devoted to the love of money, that they refuse to have normal love relationships and certainly don't want children. These people are also committed in a marriage / relationship with "love of money". Which sadly ruins young peoples lives in our generation, that by the time they "wake-up" and divorce themselves from this false materialistic pathway, they have missed the best years of their life. That too is written in the lines of one's hands, and often by living a life of mistakes in younger years helps one have a sense of true spiritual purpose in later years after making the changes to one's life .

## Lines of "Children"

The small lines rising from the marriage lines indicate children in that marriage / relationship. If these small lines are connected with the heart line, this represents that this child will have significant attachment and influence on the parents life.

## Break in Marriage Lines

In a divorce or break up of a potential marriage / love relationship there will be a break in the marriage line. This too is destiny. The lines on the hand give an indication and reassurance that this was the destiny of that relationship. Lessons needed to be learnt, and possibly Karmic as a reincarnated soul, clearance of the past was needed. Learning to release that "type" of person from one's life and learning to change one's character are necessary "heart-break" lessons for one's soul.

Wherever there is a break in a marriage line, there will always be another marriage line, seeing this indicates and gives a person reassurance that the break-up was necessary as a much more suitable relationship is waiting for one in the future.

## Straight "cold" heart line or a powerful curved wavy heart line

A straight heart line if often associated with a person who is emotionally closed and impassionate, this is especially true if the head line is more clearly defined than the heart line, which reflects they are "into" their career more than matters of the heart and love.

The more curved the heart line, the more emotional and sensual the person. People with curved lines are not afraid to demonstrate their emotions and have an intrinsically loving nature. A powerful heart line is always associated with a creative person. Whether they are an artist, builder, architect, gardener, writer, designer, fashion model, singer, songwriter, musician, inventor ... etc.

Whatever the career pathway of this person, the passionate heart line is always an excellent indication to creativity. The creative energy contained within the soul is simply an expression of loving heartfelt emotions.

**An exemplary pair of hands indicating a special person**

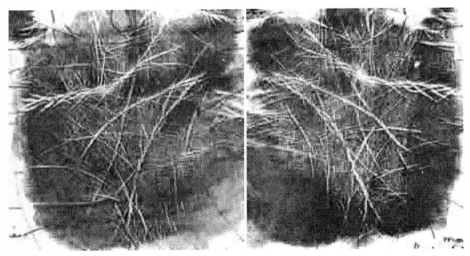

left hand                    right hand

These prints of hands are of a very famous songwriter and musician who is world famous. The soulful, meaningful words of his lyrics have had an impact on many people's lives. The amazing number of lines and strength in the lines are indicative of the strength of character of his soul. Being blessed with a passionately loving and strong character he has major imprints on his remarkable heart line. The driving force of his life is his love of people, love of life and attractive passionate nature.

From the hands above, there is a strong well defined wavy heart line, indicating a very passionate nature, with about 5 major lines going down of hateful relationships, these are indicative of leaving the strong emotional connection of abusive parents at a young age of 17 and the other problematic relationships around the age of 30. There are lines going up from the heart line, at least 6 strong relationships of which all 6 seem to be strongly emotionally committed marriages - as the lines are very strong.

The strength and depth of the heart line is indicative of the indelible affects of his creative musical career. His emotional heartfelt music holds a tremendous loving strength and passion. Musicians and love songs are often written by songwriters with a tremendously strong heart line. Creativity is just a way to express one's strong emotions.

**Destiny to learn & believe in Palmistry ONLY when your soul is ready**

It is well known that this famous person has actually had 5 strong loves so far; the next will finally be the one. That in itself has been a destiny and journey for him. As only recently did he learn about palmistry, had he learnt about palmistry before, maybe he would not have handled the relationships in the same committed way. "Destiny" and one's guardian angels will bring you the teachers and knowledge at the destined and correct time in your life.

Ones belief and spiritual understanding in the sacred knowledge of palmistry will arrive when you are spiritually ready, only when the experiences and lessons of life have been learnt. Palmistry will give one's soul the knowledge to believe that all the difficulties and experiences were destined and will give one the hope of looking forward to a lovely destined future, as one embarks on the next stage of "constructive change" of one's life.

**"I Don't Believe in Palmistry"**

For almost all young people and even old people who are not spiritually minded, when the question of Palmistry is mentioned they will have an instinctive attitude of "not believing" or a stubborn silly attitude of "not wanting" to know the "mumbo jumbo" knowledge of Palmistry, or of seeing the future ! The answer to them is simple; God would not have created the lines on one's hand if they were not meant to be studied and learnt.

The real reason why people don't want to believe in Palmistry is that once they see the truth that there is destiny created by a Divine GOD with a divine plan, this will indeed turn their materialistic selfish lives upside-down, and they will be forced to accept the need for change. Of course some people would rather leave this planet than change.

The other reason for "not wanting to believe" in Palmistry is that their souls are not ready to learn and believe, they still need to undergo pain and life situations. Only once they have had those life experiences and successfully elevated their spiritual awareness, they will then be ready to learn and understand the GOD given gift of Palmistry.

**The Head Line**

The head line runs across the palm from the area between the thumb and the forefinger, in between the heart and life lines. It deals with thinking, reasoning, the strength of one's determination and ability to focus and concentrate.

When this line is well developed, long, and straight it indicates a practical mind and success in whatever one focus' on.

**Is Your Head Line Strong?**

So with respect to one's ability to focus and change, and your strength to do so, is all seen in the strength of the HEAD LINE. If the line is strong and clear with no breaks or waves, this means you have the ability to focus and change your life, once you set your thoughts and determination to do so. People with strong head lines usually succeed and achieve their goals, aims and ambitions.

## Strong Head Line - A Determined and Good Worker

A strong headline is a sign of a hard-working, level-minded person. A short but well defined line denotes the power of concentration and determined ambition.

## Weak Head Line - Easily Distracted and Lazy

A faint or fragile looking line, whether it is short or long, tends to be associated with a mind that easily is distracted, bores with long periods of study and is prone to laziness.

## A Sloping Long Head Line and Writer's Fork

A sloping line extending from a point beneath the ring finger shows a mind that enjoys the stimulation of a variety of subjects and interests. If it slopes to a point beneath the little finger / pinky, a creative intuitive mentality is suggested. If there is a fork at the end of the head line indicates an exceedingly creative nature, normally associated with writers and musicians, the fork is actually known as the "writer's fork".

## The Fate Line

The fate line starts at the wrist and travels up the palm towards the middle finger. When it appears apart from the life line it signifies independence at an early age. The larger the gap between the head and fate line, the larger the gap between the subject and their parents. However, if there are faint lines connecting the fate line to the life line it indicates the subject will retain a good relationship with their parents. If the fate line begins as part of the life line, it suggests that the person will be strongly influenced by their parents' guidance and support early on. This by no means suggests a dependency issue because the very existence of the fate line is evidence of a person's sense of responsibility. However, when the fate line begins inside the life line, it does indicate the subject could allow their family to control them towards choice of career, and other personal matters.

## Bracelets

"Bracelets" is the name given to the two or three lines that run horizontally across the length of the wrist. Many palmists use this to determine the length of the person's life. Although in the same way the length of the life line does NOT necessarily give the number of years, but in fact indicates the number of useful and purposefully creative years of one's life.

Some old people are full of love, wisdom, kindness and helpfulness, continuing a truly useful and purposeful life even until very old age. This is indicative in the number of and strength in the lines known as "the bracelets".

Each "bracelet" line is attributed to 30 years of life span. For example; two full length bracelets and one half length bracelet would predict a lifespan of 75 years, and three full bracelets would represent 90 years.

## Changing lines

Hopefully, you now understand the basics of palmistry. It must be noted that the lines DO change, especially on one's right hand. Additional lines do appear whether they be on the heart line for good / bad relationships, whether they be on the head line for focused determination, career changes etc , or all over the palm of the hand on mounds of the finger, which we explain more in our book "Yad Palmistry" due out in Summer 2006.

## 2. Palmistry teaches that each person is unique

When one understands that the strength and individuality of one's' soul is contained within the precision of each of the lines of one's hands, this opens up a door in one's mind and soul to the importance of recognizing this perfect precision of Palmistry that GOD has created our physical body with a perfect exactness and is a reflection of our soul, so that each and every line our hands are perfectly accurate.

## The Physical Body is a mirror reflection of the Spiritual Soul

ספר חובת הלבבות In the Book Chovos Halevovos by Rabeinu Ibn Paquida known as "Duties of the Heart" in the Chapter Shaar Bechina explains that our bodies were created with the finest of detail and precision. Every mark, every colour and shape on our body is a reflection of our soul that is contained within that body.

That is the reason why the colour of one's eyes is so important spiritually, as our eyes are considered the windows of our soul, light coloured eyes such as green & blue eyes, reflect a souls radiance of spiritual healing and knowledge of a creative higher level, whereas brown, black and dark eyes indicate a soul of lower and darker earthly energy.

## The "Spiritual Healing Hands" A Potential Gift to EVERY Human

חובת הלבבות writes that GOD, the Divine Creator of all life on earth, created the human body in such a way that the hands are not only useful in physical acts, but have an equal and more important role spiritually . Of course there are people who do not believe in palmistry or do not even want to know of the spiritual power of the hands. The simple reason they do not believe the spiritual beliefs and in palmistry is because their soul is NOT ready to believe and understand spiritual aspects. Sadly, for many people they will live their whole earthly life never believing, nonetheless GOD has blessed EVERY individual with the POTENTIAL to awaken their soul.

## Look at your hands

חובת הלבבות writes that every person should take a few minutes every day looking at the lines on the palms of one's hands. Giving thanks to GOD for blessing us with this detailed map of our souls destined pathway in life, and praying that we should understand the lines on our hands, and succeed to live to our fullest spiritual potential.

As you look and stare at the palms of your hands, consider the fact that you are communicating with your own soul. Reflect on the fact that NO ONE in the whole world has the same set of lines on their hands as you. The energy and character of your soul is in the palms of your hands.

When you look at your hands, answer these questions: - "Do you like the lines on your hands and what you see about yourself?" "Is it peaceful and comforting to stare at your own hands?" The answers to these questions reflect how you feel about yourself spiritually.

### 4. The Power of Ones Soul is in Ones Hands

Understanding that the hands are the most powerful connection between one's physical existence and one's spiritual soul, everyone's hands hold the key to one's spirituality. Using the power contained within one's hands and soul brings healing, positive energy, inner spiritual and physical strengthening. Leading to an understanding of the true power of praying with one's hands, shaking hands, holding hands, saluting, clapping, and using one's hands to protect one's souls and keep one's soul and aura clean

# The Priests Blessing ברכת כהנים

## יברכך ה וישמרך
## יאר ה פניו אליך ויחנך
## פניו אליך וישם לך שלום ישא ה

The "Kohanim" Jewish Priests held their hands in this way for the priestly blessing. In fact they held their hands with the thumbs together so that the two hands together looked like 5 points outwards. As tradition of kabbala is never to draw the exactness of the image as it is sacred.

The first mention of blessing with the power of one's hands, that is giving someone a spiritual blessing, transferring energy through the power of one's hands is in Genesis chapter 48 verse 14, when Jacob blesses his grandchildren, Ephraim and Menashe. From the times when the Torah was given at Mount Sinai, the priests KOHANIM, where chosen as dedicated servants of GOD for the temple, as it was the whole tribe of Levi that did not worship the Golden Calf, in fact symbolic that they did not worship materialism, and therefore most suitable for a wholesome and perfect spiritual life.

Hence continues the tradition today, every Friday night parents bless their children by placing their hands on top of their heads. Similarly Rebbes, spiritual Rabbis place their hands on a persons head when blessing them.

The energy of the soul is communicated to the palms of one's hands, giving a person by placing the hands on a persons head transfers spiritually the blessing from their soul.

## Position of Hands to be focused and closed

During prayers and whenever one needs focused concentration, then one needs to be closed to outside influences clasp one's hands together as in the picture above. As the Talmud explains, there are

95

times when we need to be completely closed to external bad influences, the need for closure is not just a physical need, in order to protect one's life from criminals, but one also needs to have one's soul closed to spiritual thieves who attempt to steal energy from one's soul.

Our hands are the external connection between the physical world and our spiritual soul, hence by closing one's fists and clasping both hands together, closes one's soul to the external world.

**Praying hands**

The correct spiritual position for maximizing one's soulful prayers with effect is as in the diagram above. According to Kabbala only the fingertips and bottom of one's palms should be touching. Try praying whilst holding one's hands in this spiritual praying position and feel the difference from within your soul.

## Shaking Hands

The act of shaking hands is an exceedingly spiritual experience, shaking hands connects two people spiritually. Their souls are connected very strongly by the handshake. Hence many spiritually minded people are exceedingly careful with whom they shake hands.

## Holding Hands

Understanding that shaking hands makes a soulful connection, this therefore emphasizes the importance of husband and wife holding hands. Even if they have had an argument or have a problem, if they can hold hands then there souls will reconnect without all the materialistic egos getting involved. Simply by holding hands a man and a woman will have a spiritual connection with each other and feel the true love.

If a man and woman cannot hold hands this reflects that there souls are not connected with each other. It would probably be a good idea for all young couples to meet simply by shaking and holding hands to see and sense spiritually if they are compatible with each other. As this was actually the tradition as quoted in Talmud Taanis 31a, they used to choose their wives & husbands by looking at the spiritually qualities of their souls and not the external superficial beauty or wealth . By making a soulful connection their relationships were safe and secure based on destiny of meeting their true soulmate.

## Saluting

Saluting is also a very spiritual act, as the raising of one's hand to greet another, showing the palms of one's hand to the fellow soldier, as if to say he is to be trusted and comes with an open soul, with nothing to hide, this is a spiritual act of greeting in peace.

## Clapping

As we explained the two hands represent to sides of our character, the right hand - the side of kindness חסד, the left hand - the side of strength גבורה . Indeed the act of clapping is considered a spiritual act whereby the soul connects these two qualities with strength of clapping, in so doing clapping actually cleanses any bad vibrations away from the person's soul. Try clapping one's hands as one is sitting in traffic and feel the relief of tension! It was actually an oriental custom to clap when one wakes up in the morning to cleanse one's soul.

## Using one's hands to protect one's soul

Understanding that one's strength of one's soul is in the palms of one's hands. Use the palms of one's hands to push away any negativity. Simply place your hand in front of you and push the negativity away with the palms of one's hands pushing outwards.

## Hands that Heal a Headache

Whenever a person has a headache there is always a tendency to hold one's head with one's hands . This is instinctively and subconsciously what everyone does, to use their hands and hence their souls energy to bring healing and strength to their head. Likewise for any hurt, ache or pain the instinctive reaction is to place your hand on that wounded or hurt part of your body.

## Keeping one's hands clean

With this new knowledge and spiritual awareness that the hands are the physical extensions of one's soul, this emphasizes how crucial it is to keep one's hands clean. Washing one's hand is indeed a spiritual act of washing and cleansing one's soul.

# Chapter 11

## The Stages of Change in Life

"Every day a spiritual voice announces to the whole world to wake up...and change"

But are you in tune? Are you sensitive enough to hear this voice every day? Do you hear the need to change? Do you feel uncomfortable and have that inner feeling that your life is NOT in order? Do you feel that need to change for the better?

### The Seven Stages of Life

The physical growth during our lives is simply a reflection of our spiritual growth as the levels of one's soul enter the physical body. As we grow and mature physically through these stages, we transform and change. In each period of our lives a different set of parameters/ rules apply. It would be inconceivable that a 30 year old should behave with the same way a baby behaves, although we all know some people who never seem to grow up!

### 1. Infancy & Early Childhood 0 to 7 years old

Learning to survive, relying totally on the people around, copying and emulating everyone. The survival of the first seven years is based totally, in receiving energy from others by any means possible, crying, demanding, cheating and deception, or more subtly through loving and being sweet. Whatever technique is applied to receiving from the adult world, this leaves a lasting impression on one's soul and is carried forward into adult life, unless changed by reprogramming this behavioral pattern.

In this infancy stage a baby reacts naturally, when something hurts and pains the immediate reaction is to cry. Crying clears the negative energy so much that the infant will almost immediately forget the pain after a good cry. Crying is not only a way of attracting attention, but an inner spiritual reaction to dissolving the negative hurt. The child will also immediately forgive the hurt or damage and will never harbour any resentment.

As adults, we forget this normal reaction that we were supposed to have learnt, and fight the pain by suppressing the hurt feelings. Until the hurt becomes too much to cope with and affects the health of the adult. It would therefore be an excellent idea if we would learn from this infant stage, and cry whenever there is hurt instead of suppressing the negative emotions and forgive and forget immediately, instead of harbouring resentment jealousy bitterness, all the negative emotions that prevent us living as complete and wholesome adults with lovely purposeful lives.

## 2. Childhood 7 - 15 years old

The emergence of the personality and copied identity, during these years a person, still impressed and sensitive to emulate the people, the mannerisms and character of those they come into contact with, start to develope their own individualistic character.

This character is based entirely on the influences that the child comes into contact with. If the child is brought up by a nanny and the television, the parents must expect to see a confused child of our modern society. If the child is brought up by kind intelligent educated, thoughtful and loving parents, whom allow the child to be impressed by their etiquette and decency. The child will indeed copy the identity of those parents.

These years of education and transformation of character are the basis of the adult life. If in later years the adult has made mistakes and erred, it is because the foundation of one's character in these years was poor. Hence in reforming and changing one's nature in later years, imperatively one needs to look at the influences of these childhood years. De- brainwashing and reprogramming all the false copied characteristics one was impressed during childhood.

As Dr Carl Jung, the eminent Swiss psychologist says inherently no person is bad or evil, it is simply their soul and character has been tainted by bad influences. Everyone is intrinsically good, and has the potential to accomplish greatness and goodness with love, kindness and sincerity.

### 3. Adolescence, 15 until 21-26 years old

The element of one's soul known as the Ruach רוח, enters one's physical life and spiritual soul during these years. This essence of one's spirit soul Ruach is the power of speech. The power of speech allows a person to communicate one's inner thoughts from one's soul to another person. Thereby creating energy whether it has constructive, through intelligent, kind and loving words, or destructive, through lies, deceit and slander. This period of one's life allows the adolescent to explore these energies, both constructive and destructive.

The inner hormonal changes, peer groups, doubts and questions, help the adolescent refine and develope an individuality of character. Exploring life helps the young adult find one's own individualistic identity, values and purpose in life. During this transition from childhood to adulthood, one may feel disorientated, especially, if the basis in childhood was incorrect. A level of insecurity comes with the changing adolescent, until one learns to have self confidence.

If indeed a person has had to undergo a complete life change in later years, the insecurity during that change is the insecurity of the adolescent, until confidence in the self is gained by having the strength of character, to intrinsically know that all is now repaired within one's soul. This is especially true after a divorce, where the honest person questions one's life pathway and has many adolescent doubts and lacks a self confidence.

If the characteristics taught in the childhood stage and carried forward in this period were hateful, selfish and materialistic, the young adult will continue with this basis in life, surviving by developing a ruthless and selfish character. It may take many years before something happens to awaken the person to the truth, or the person may actually continue along this pathway and then straight into old age - a living death, without any consideration for anything as profound as a spiritual soul.

## 4. Adulthood - from adolescence until 30-45 years old

Adulthood is the creative period of one's life. This stage allows all the lessons and foundations of one's character that one has developed to then assume a responsible role in life.

Marriage and sexual intimacy for the purpose of creating loving energy and having children., at this stage one has transformed one's nature from a taker of energy, to a creator and giver of loving and supportive energy .

Ones career and purpose in life are formed in this period, and an identity label of whom you are is formed. This identity is based on your foundations of the earlier stages and guided by your values your set yourself during adolescence.

The achievements in one's life during this period identify who the person is and are simply a reflection of the inner soul. If compared to a budding flower some radiate beauty, colour scent and aroma whilst some simply grow leaves and seeds. Nonetheless everyone has an individualistic and unique purpose and identity, the fruits of one's earlier stages of life.

## 5. The Mid Life Crisis, from 26 - 45 years old until the end of life

This period is exceedingly important, and happens to everyone. Some people choose to ignore their feelings, suppressing any need for change, and settle themselves into directly into old age - a selfish life without use or creative purpose. However, most people, use these feelings sensibly to either make slight alterations to their lives or turn their useless lives upside-down starting afresh and building solid foundations.

During the mid-life crisis years, a person will have dissatisfaction with attainments in life; and will have a growing awareness of physical decline and mortality. Experiencing down-in-the-dumps depressing moments, with feelings that the life they wanted and dreamt of is not as expected, the vitality and sense of loving creative purpose they had imagined as a child is not there, and there seems to be a hollow vacuum. This stage of life will have the emphasis on a search for truth, meaning and purpose of life.

Having pursued with vigour the desires, wishes and fantasies of a teenager, by the mid life crisis years, the honest person will realize that these were the wishes and desires of an immature teenager. Now with the wisdom of experience, the gift of intuition, strength of an adult and with honesty, the individual confronts the innermost feelings. Knowing that getting-it-right will lead to a wholesome and golden stage of life. Getting it wrong will lead to a premature living death.

Hence it becomes an emergency to CHANGE, at all costs, even at the expense of status in life, if the job is depressing and draining then there is no other option than to quit the job or business or at the expense of divorce, especially if one realizes that the husband/wife isn't even one's soulmate. These are some of the drastic measures we know people in mid-life experience and are perfectly normal.

Recognizing the uselessness and wastefulness of the earlier years, may lead some to fall into a depression or even worse try escape tactics, and that includes getting on with life as usual by suppressing the feelings one's souls is trying to express. This occurs as one may feel the changes in one's life are simply too overwhelming to do, and other people may get hurt upset or offended, especially spouses whom do not comprehend this stage in life and refuse to be supportive or change, preferring to have security in the status quo instead of an improved spiritual and purposeful life.

However, after a period of sulking and feeling sorry for oneself, analyzing the worst scenarios, the sensible person recognizes the need for transformation.

This time of transformation, is always accompanied by reminiscing the childhood and adolescent years. This is instinctively done by the soul, as a way to help identify the lost mid-life crisis person where they went wrong.

The root cause for not having a perfect and wholesome life is that the foundations laid were of poor quality. By uprooting those bad foundations and laying new one's, based on spiritual, purposeful, loving and creative values, the person transforms the inherent childhood and adolescent stages that were engrained, (and in some cases brainwashed) by misinformed and misguided parents. One then learns to be one's own parent, laying foundations based on one's own personal experiences and mistakes.

When a movie director makes a film, the director has a very clear end vision fixed in their head. The director will use his/her experience insights and knowledge to keep going over the same scene until its 100% correct. Similarly the honest adult in mid-life crisis will keep on making the corrections until the perfect end vision that one's soul and Guardian Angels can see is fulfilled. However, painful and boring it maybe to keep going over the same scene, the persons soul realizes that unless it is perfect, they will not be able to live with the uncomfortable feelings of a lack of purpose and void in life.

## 6. The Golden Age, from mid life crisis years until old age

This period is ONLY applicable to those people whom have worked on themselves during the mid-life crisis years, refining their character with spiritual meaning of life. This person now has a life of creative purpose based on kindness, love and spiritual understanding.

The person radiates and exudes life and vitality. It is said that many successful 40 year olds look younger that some old aged 30 year olds. Having attained the goal of realigning their principles ideals and goals in life, they are given an amazing new lease of life. Having discarded all the draining situations out of their lives, they are only left with good friends of similar purposeful lives.

In this GOLDEN period, comes a maturity and knowledge that all of life is interrelated in a cycle of life and loving energy; there is no shortage nor scarcity of love, as love is created by one's thoughts and actions and abundance runs freely in one's life. One becomes and exudes contentment with whatever one has, one no longer forces life to happen and a serenity of peacefulness, harmony and calmness reigns.

As the person radiates these feelings, goodness and happiness are now attracted into the person's life magically and magnetically.

To the person who has been blessed with the stage of "Golden Age" then the next stage of old age may only last a few weeks or even a few hours to a truly righteous person, whom have fulfilling lives until the day one dies.

### 7. Old age, possibly from 30 years old on

This period of old age is the acceptance that one's productive creative years have ended, and that the person no longer has anything to offer of any purpose to other people.

The confrontation of eventual death, together with the fact that the person has no spiritual values, they can become more materialistic and selfish, with fears of lack that they will not have enough money in later years. They become ruthless and arrogantly selfish, in complete atheistic denial that there is a GOD or any form of belief on life-after-death.

These people survive life, by using the power of creative speech to lie and destroy other people's lives. As they intrinsically know their lives are lost and wasted, so ruthlessly they desire to destroy as many good people along with them, by their deceit and manipulation.

The sincerely good people, who are living in an enlightened spiritual "Golden Age" of their lives, sense this and see through these types of people, keeping a safe distance away from them. Usually after the midlife crisis years, we find groups of people whom have polarized themselves into either constructive creative people with a life energy and vitality of the "Golden Age" and another group of the arrogant selfish and materialistic living dead at the "OLD AGE" stage of life. There is simply no inbetween.

Sadly for those whom have resigned themselves not to change in their mid-life crisis, they have chosen by their freewill to be selfish and not to give to others, they have committed spiritual suicide on themselves. They have chosen to disconnect from the eternal Divine life energy of GOD, and hence survive by stealing life energy from other people, which after a time all the intrinsically good people feel a "draining energy" when connected with these people.

These people have a real fear of death and eventually leave this world with no idea or spiritual preparation for what waits. Once they have died, they are soon forgotten, as they have left nothing of any purpose or use in their selfish lives.

Although old age can start at 30, for women this can occur earlier, in particular those women who choose not to have, lack any wish or desire to have children. Similarly men who have operations to prevent them having children, they have disconnected with the creative life energy. They have brought selfish old age upon themselves, of course this pathway of self destruction can be stopped at any moment by simply waking up spiritually.

**Life Changes Can Occur at Anytime**

Now that we understand that life has 7 stages, we shall now introduce the idea of 5 stages of change. Change can occur during ANY stage of life, at anytime, can take a year or 10 years, there is no time limit set on change, it is up to the ability of one's soul to cope with and transform.

Nonetheless the person usually goes through a reflective period in their lives during the mid-life crisis years, which acts as a catalyst of change, at that stage of life one can reflect clearly and with enough experiences of life, to make the right corrections to change life into a fulfilling and purposeful life.

106

## The 5 Stages of Life Transformation

Change can be easy; by changing your thoughts, you change your feelings, and thus change your actions and events in your life. In our generation, we have better skills to deal with problems and situations, as we are more enlightened and aware than ever before in history.

Even still, it often has to get darker before it becomes lighter and brighter. In our modern world, we do not need to wait until something happens to cause us to change. In fact, you can choose to live a change oriented, rich, and fulfilling life right NOW. To transform your life, you need to raise your awareness, practice pro-activity, and live by your vision, purpose, and values.

"There is nothing about a caterpillar that tells you it's going to be a butterfly", this quote from the famous Tiferes Yisroel, Reb Yisroel Lipschitz in his book "Derush Ohr HaChayim" explaining the ability to simply have faith during any process and stage of change in one's life. He illustrates the change process perfectly as a butterfly represents a thing of great beauty. A butterfly completely transforms itself from a caterpillar into a comfortable cocoon then into a radiant entity with wings. You are like a beautiful butterfly waiting to be re-born and transformed. Don't be frightened of change!

### *Stage 1: Cocoon Stage*

This stage is characterized by feelings of comfort, as you are beginning to awaken to the need to change. You begin to realize you could be so much more and recognize an error in judgment or dysfunctional pattern(s).

### *Stage 2: Growth Stage*

This stage is characterized by feelings of discomfort, as you are beginning to stretch yourself, your abilities, and your environment. You experience new ways of being and thinking and have the desire to transform yourself.

### *Stage 3: Change Stage*

This stage is characterized by feelings of panic and fear, as you are beginning to look, feel, and act differently. You have a gut instinct that this change will be good for you and request that Spirit and your Guardian Angels assist you to provide with you with reassurance signs and guidance.

Nonetheless, during this stage, you may feel like your whole life is falling and has fallen apart, the only hope being sadness, loneliness, death and misery, you will probably be extremely fragile and sensitive. Just think of the caterpillar transforming into the butterfly, trust that you are changing and suddenly when the time is right you will come alive, with a brighter and more fulfilled life.

### *Stage 4: Flight Stage*

This stage is characterized by feelings of confidence and courage, as you spread your wings to leave your old home to find a new home. You now recognize yourself as a beautiful creature, have excitement about future possibilities and you just do it.

### *Stage 5: Conscious Stage*

This stage is characterized by feelings of inner peace and joy, as you remember and realize who you really are. You now understand that you are a co-creator and possess the power to become whatever you want to be and do whatever you want to do.

# Explanation of Stage 3: The Change Stage

During the "change stage" certain feelings and happenings will occur mysteriously which will make a person feel extremely sensitive and unsettled. I shall discuss these specific events here in order to reassure the reader that these events happen. They are perfectly normal in everyone's life, during the "change stage".

## Feeling alone

Appropriate relationships, the demands of your life during this period of transformation, will force you to reevaluate which relationships in your life are worth keeping and which are not.

If you do not face this challenge consciously, then events will occur that will force you too to do so. Even people who have been with you for a long time will leave against your wishes.

Suddenly you will find yourself feeling alone and out of touch with everybody. You may feel you have no support from others, even loved one's whom you have counted on in the past for love and support. Even people whom you have helped and supported in the past suddenly are not there, now that you need help.

This breakdown in relationships is perfectly normal, whilst a person is changing. Think of a person like a spider on a spiders web, before the person can move on to a new home and a new life, it is vitally necessary to detach oneself from the present entanglements, when the last disconnection is made , one maybe exceedingly fragile and lonely, but now one is free to move anywhere .

This influence of change is likely to have a very disruptive effect on your relationships. Influences may enter your life during this stage that will challenge the foundations upon which your life is built. This challenge will be reflected in surprising encounters with others that upset your way of living or in sudden separations from persons who you thought would always be in your life.

During this period, it is quite likely that you will do things and go places you never would have thought of in the past. Anyone who is wedded to the status quo in life or to their past, will find this influence exceedingly disturbing and difficult.

Even one's true love and aspirations of romance will change. In false romance that pursues purely animalistic passions and desires, the lower sexual-drive energies predominate. As with all materialistic and animals desires, this urge and attraction wears-off with time.

True love and romance is open hearted, heart centered full of emotions based on truth, love and sincerity. True romance utilizes the energy of one's soul. As we explain in the chapter on Soulmates as one connects with one's soulmate, the spiritual energy created in the connection will bring you both very close to each other. On a level of telepathy, one knows exactly what the other one is thinking and feeling. There is indeed a sense of wholesomeness as each knows they are each others half, feeling the pain and joy of the other person.

During the transformation stage of mid-life crisis, one may look to deepen one's relationship with one's spouse rising to this spiritual level OR one may indeed be going through a divorce in search of one's true soulmate and destiny. Recognizing that one's current spouse is NOT one's true destiny is another difficult decision to make during the transitional change stage.

**Understanding that All Changes in Life Happen for Good - So be Calm and Trust.**

בהרחבת הדעת ומנוחת הנפש

This is my blessing (ברכה Brucha), to you in our generation of changes, to wish everyone tranquility and peace of mind. Learn to accept the tests, challenges and changes in our life with peace of mind, calmness and acceptance from GOD.

There is nothing wrong in having made mistakes in one's youth, provided one is honest in mid-life to admit the mistakes, and change for the better. It is well known that one of the greatest Rabbis - Rabbi Akiva only began his spiritual learning at the age of 40.

Learn to trust in GOD and spirit world, take life calmly, accepting everything that happens is for the best. In acknowledging the fact that one's life was on the wrong pathway, needs courage and strength of character to leave the past in the past and move on to the future.

Whilst changes are occurring, trust and know that there is a divine plan for you and that nothing happens by accident or coincidence.

Everything will turn out just fine for you in your life and you too will arrive at the golden stage of, radiating the glow of a purposeful life, of loving kindness, aliveness and vitality. It will happen for you, just like it has happened for millions of people before you on our planet, created by GOD for a purposeful, creative life of love and change.

**Our destiny and purpose in this life is to change.**

Life on planet earth is constantly changing; the flowers, trees, animal kingdom and even the most stubborn of human beings who resist change are changing.

Consider a tree during the seasons; does the tree resist change during the autumn months as the leaves fall off? We all understand that this is a cycle of life, the tree has not died, simply taking a rest during the winter, before it reinvents itself and grows longer and bigger in the spring.

עוּרוּ עוּרוּ משׁׁינתכם

**So Wake Up, Be Brave and Change**

Embrace life and the wonderful changes that will transform your life !

# Chapter 12

## Ability to Make Changes in Ones Life

מַה שֶּׁלֹּא יַעֲשֶׂה הַשֵּׂכֶל .... יַעֲשֶׂה הַזְּמָן

"For everything that the intellect cannot accomplish then time will succeed to accomplish", philosophy of life's changes quoted from Sefer Shinuyim.

### Teaching a child to walk

Every single baby learns to walk; this is a simple fact of life. The young child does not take lessons in walking nor goes to a school where walking is taught.

The child learns by itself, the child looks, observes and tries to copy the adults it sees. It sees everyone in the world standing up on two feet, so it has a vision that it is possible, and more importantly, the child is 100% certain that it will soon be able to stand on two feet just like everyone else .

Instinctively we know that there is "nothing new under the sun". Our life experiences have been experienced by someone somewhere in the world, and hence when we are looking for help, we look for someone whom has experienced life, someone who has been through everything and succeeded in life's challenges.

However painful and however many times the child falls down and even hurts itself, the child will NEVER give up the pursuit of learning to walk. This is our lesson for our lives. Every change eventually happens, it is just a matter of time, hence the expression

מה שלא יעשה השכל .... יעשה הזמן

"For everything that the intellect cannot accomplish then time will succeed to accomplish", it's just a matter of time, of course there are some things that are not meant to happen and no matter how much time they will never happen, the wisdom is to know what can be and what cant be changed.

## Confidence, Faith & Trust

All levels of change are basically similar experiences, just on different levels. In hindsight anyone who has been through each stage successfully looks back and sees how simple the stage was. Like a anyone who reflects on early stages of trying to walk as a baby or riding a bicycle, will laugh at the fact that there was a time when they kept falling down. "There's nothing new under the sun"

Likewise every stage of life one is currently experiencing, there is 100% certainty that someone has experienced this before. Whether it be the insecurity of finding a job, finding love, responsibility and commitment of marriage, trauma or relief of divorce, death of a loved one or simply a mid-life crisis, in which one feels a fool that one has wasted one's life pursuing a futile selfish existence and one wants to change, but thinks it will be too messy and difficult. Every possible and conceivable difficult situation has been experienced by someone somewhere before you; they succeeded in changing so this should reassure you that you too can succeed. For example, when one goes through a divorce believing that one will never find love again, it is accepted fact of life that everyone whom has loved once will love again.

The main reason a person fails is because of a lack of self confidence and belief in one's abilities. If we look at every situation in life and compare it to a child learning to walk, we should feel reassured that EVERY PROBLEM has a SOLUTION, provided we stay focused, learn the lessons of the experience properly, take good advice in overcoming the difficulties. Most importantly we MUST have the strength and confidence that we will succeed, and that destiny will be fulfilled with a trust and confidence in GOD that everything will be fine.

## What are the reasons for a lack of self-confidence?

The lack of self confidence is the single most important reason why people fail in life. The reasons for this malady of lack of self-confidence are simple: -

"Brainwashing" - from an early age one's parents, deceitful friends and maybe the community or society one lives in, have constantly been giving hammering into one's mind and thoughts messages of "not being good enough", people have acted independently but collectively to destructively criticize one's life, highlight one's mistakes and never compliment or focus on one's achievements.

This is especially true for children of parents who do not believe in GOD or values of love and kindness. Often children brought up by abusive parents are very sensitive and lack confidence because of their parents' negativity, fears, abuse, bullying and intimidation. Such children need to get away from such draining and evil parents, with a need to gain a self confidence, realizing that all the abusive brainwashing was their parents problem and "baggage" and nothing to do with them.

Modern competitive society, also sends us messages of "not being good enough", whether it be our physical appearance or our financial materialistic status that require us to go out and buy the latest gimmick gadgets to keep up with our friends as status symbol of the materialistic society .

Simply eliminate all the brainwashing and destructive critical messages sent to our brain and soul over all the years can undo the damage done. Don't be afraid of failure, A lot of good failures are the main ingredient in the recipe for success. Mistakes are the greatest of life's teachers, so what if you fail - you can always try again!

We are not born perfect and the vast majority of people will not die perfect. We are expected to make mistakes in our lives. The more fruitful a person's life has become, is a sign that they have made more mistakes, learnt by their mistakes and are no longer afraid of failure.

They live life to the fullest potential, unlike the opposite kind of person that does nothing constructive with their lives because they are constantly afraid of failure.

Every person in the whole world makes mistakes, this is completely normal, in fact the more mistakes a person makes, provided the person makes the corrections, then the greater the person can become.

**"If you don't try - you won't succeed"**

This well known saying teaches the message, if one is frightened of living and frightened of failure, one is missing the chance of success. So what if you fail the first time and again at the second time, there is the saying "THIRD TIME LUCKY!"

Once accepts failure as a fact of life, and learns the lessons of failure, no longer being frightened of failure, by being honest with oneself, then one elevates one's character and soul with strength, courage and bravery that one can achieve anything, even and especially when other challenging people still continue to be destructively critical that the venture will fail, one can succeed!

The strong and courageous person will continue to try and succeed, as their comments of his/her enemies are given no energy and negated altogether. The experience of failure one time will lead to success the next time. A well known fact is that most self-made millionaires have failed in at least two businesses in the past. They have used their experiences to finally create success.

**A Guarantee for Success** בתר רישא גופא אזיל

"Following the start, the main part follows", this spiritual principle has deep meaning, the start of each week is Sunday, day one of creation. The energy and actions one does on a Sunday reflects the type of week one is going to have. If one sleeps in having wasted the Saturday night in futile activities of TV or going out then one can only expect a sleepy and wasteful week.

Use each and every Sunday to get one's mind thoughts and soul in a good attitude and energized to handle the forthcoming week with courage and energy to change one's life. Utilizing the first day of the week in creative activity, of goodness, kindness and love will set the foundations for the whole week to be energized and alive, and be able to break the destructive cycle of weekly events, especially the bad influences of other people's problems.

**Change by Generating your own Inner Confidence**

Set the foundation of your new changed character based on spiritual truth, think of all the good things you have done in your life, impressed upon your soul, and don't listen to the false allegations that other people have attempted to dump onto your soul.

Speak to yourself with honesty and encouragement. Contemplate on all the peoples lives you have helped and how their lives would be different if you would not have been there to help. Congratulate yourself constructively for all your good deeds.

One of the reasons why we love to help others is the feeling of purpose and aliveness that comes from the joy of being appreciated. So start by showing yourself appreciation and thanking yourself for all the goodness you have done. Especially, if you have done much for ungrateful people, whom will never appreciate what you have done; compensate their bad negative attitude for your words of encouragement to yourself. This will infuse energy within your soul to flow a continuity of happiness and satisfaction to make yourself feel appreciated and help you to continue doing good deeds, in spite of what horrible people say about you.

**Faith & Trust in GOD as GOD will make a way where there is no way**

A person feels confident with themselves when they know that they are behaving correctly in life, with kindness, faith, love and trust in GOD. When a person knows that they are good in the eyes of GOD, no matter what anyone gossips about them, it simply does not matter as GOD and spirit world know the truth.

Living with this faith and trust in GOD will bring a person self reassurance that GOD will make a correct and protected way for you in your life even where there seems to be no way .

## Keep Your Intentions Secret

אין הברכה חל אלא על דבר הסמוי מן העין

"A true blessing only starts upon something that is hidden from the eye and private", in spirit law until an action is done, other peoples negative thoughts can cancel out your thoughts and plans. The one time you can break this rule is if you absolutely must tell just your mum or best friend, presuming they sincerely have your best interests at heart!

Even some friends and relatives, still have a jealousy factor, if you are more successful, happy, lucky or richer than they. They are only human, and if they have missed their life's chances, then they may have a bitterly jealous nature to see you succeed. So keep quiet and tell no one as you are changing, and by listening to your Guardian Angels following your plans you will be able to change your life successfully and find your true purpose and destiny in life.

# Chapter 13

## The Power of Prayer and asking for Divine help

### Focusing Ones Thoughts In Successful Prayer

The power of one's thoughts and the power of prayer have always had and continue to have the potential to change every possible situation; it all depends of the strength of one's FOCUS in one's mind, thoughts and soul.

### Introduction

Every living person in this world thinks of 1000's of thoughts every day. Most of our thoughts do not have any energy, purpose, strength, nor do they have any affects on anyone's lives whatsoever. However, when a person learns how to develope a focused thought energy, then a person will be able to use the power of a single thought to change one's life, and rectify any difficult or problematic situations in one's life.

It is ONLY the power of our thoughts that can change our lives. Once we learn how to master and control our thoughts then we are able to be in control of our lives, and then we are able to find our true successful and purposeful destiny for our soul's physical journey of life on earth.

### 1. What is a Thought מחשבה ?

A thought is the most pure of spiritual energy we can create in this physical world with our physical mind, body and spiritual soul. Everything in this world that we accomplish with our physical bodies and spiritual souls can be categorized into one of 3 groups:-

## Thoughts, Spoken Words & Actions

A thought is the most spiritual of energy one can create with one's mind and soul. The thought then has the potential to become a spoken word, if one decides to give the thought physical energy. The thought also has the potential to become an action directly or as a result of the spoken word.

THOUGHTS are SPIRITUAL, they are messages you send out and create from within your soul, and messages that your soul receives from spirit world or from other people that you are sensitive and intune with, thoughts are the spiritual communication within one's soul to other people's soul and to the eternal Divine spiritual realms.

WORDS have the capacity to be both SPIRITUAL and PHYSICAL. Words start the process of converting pure spiritual thought energy into a physical existence in this world. Words express the physical result of actions with either approval or disapproval, and act to continue the cycle of the thought process. Words are then used to make changes if the action proved a failure or words are used positively to confirm that the action was successful.

ACTIONS are PHYSICAL. They are a result of thoughts being converted into a physical action, either directly from the thought or by way of spoken word.

## Thoughts Connect Ones Soul Spiritually

Thoughts are the most spiritual entity that we can create in this physical world, therefore, it is a thought from within our mind and soul that has the power to connect our soul to the eternal DIVINE spiritual realms.

A thought energy is the spiritual energy that connects us with our Guardian Angels and with anyone or any soul with whom our spiritual thought energy has the ability to connect with, depending on the energy from within our soul and the energy of the soul in "Spirit world" that wishes to help us.

## The Prayer Cycle

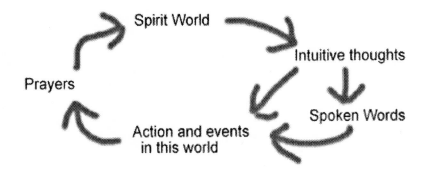

The prayer cycle which in reality is simply the spiritual creative life cycle of all existence at the highest level attainable by humans on earth, explains the concepts of thoughts, words and actions interrelating with each other.

When actions or events happen in this world that we do not like, we immediately express ourselves by complaining or praying. If we choose to complain then these words are wasted.

If we choose to pray with positive thoughts and sensible reasoning, accepting the reality of the situation in our lives, and genuinely desiring to know why "things went wrong", then these words and thoughts are channeled to spirit world correctly.

Every prayer is heard when we focus our words, thoughts and even our tears as tears create a very strong spiritual energy to elevate our thoughts to spirit world.

When the time is right, the spiritual help transcends into our life as intuitive thoughts, good ideas and instinctive guidance. When the transcending of spiritual energy is strong, it can transcend into other peoples thoughts influencing them to help and even cause events "divine coincidences" and spiritual miracles to occur.

## A Prayer Without Thinking is a Waste of Time!

"Whether a person prays a lot or prays a little - then most important aspect that when one prays one thinks and concentrates one's prayer to GOD"

Many people ask "why aren't my prayers answered?" Answer is simple - a prayer that has no "thought" energy attached to it is a waste of time. It is better to pray for 1 minute a day with concentration than to "say & chant prayers" for hours without no thought energy! Successful prayer is about QUALITY - not quantity!

## GOD will make a way, where there seems to be no way

The experience of living in this world is to come to a stage in life to admit that one cannot work everything out and one needs Divine help. Admitting this truth when one is in a seemingly unsolvable situation and praying "Please GOD make a way for me where there seems to be no way", is not just a last resort but a method to accept Divine spiritual help in one's life, that's the purpose of praying to ask and receive help.

## Simple and Effective Prayers

"Dear God: Although I have ignored You for all these years and even denied Your existence, and not appreciated all You have done for me, I'm in trouble now"

## Writing a Prayer Request

There is a famous Jewish spiritual tradition from Sefer Shinuyim, the Book of Changes, that is to write a prayer request before going to sleep at night and to sleep with this paper under your pillow, or hold the paper in one's hand as one falls asleep.

Write down your prayer and your request for help on a pieces of paper before you go to sleep and address it to your Guardian Angels to help you.

This is very powerful, and one will feel the amazing difference in the morning with some intuitive answers. Keep writing down your feelings and sleeping with this paper under your pillow, or in your hand for as long as you feel you need.

Within 30 days you will feel the change, coincidences and answers will come your way. And always remember to THANK GOD and your Guardian Angels.

## Light a Candle Anytime

Whenever you feel the need for some extra special spiritual help or if you genuinely wish to thank your Guardian Angels at anytime for their help that has been given then light a candle and pray. Likewise when you pray for the future of world, for peace, love and spiritual growth of all of mankind, light a candle and pray at anytime of any day.

## Closing one's eyes and praying

By closing one's physical eyes, one is closing the physical materialistic world out of one's mind, and makes it so much easier to focus on the purest Spiritual thoughts and the ability to pray and have one's prayers answered comes much easier when one closes one's eyes.

# Chapter 14

### "A single thought has the power to change the whole world"

### Sefer Shinuyim ספר שינוים

## Using one's mind, thoughts and soul
## to create changes in one's life

The most important aspect in learning to live a successful life is always to remain positive and to think positive about everything that happens. Understanding the strength of "positive thinking" is simply having the correct attitude, mind and soul full of good energizing thoughts.

Problems and difficult situations will keep on happening in our lives, but the way we look at life according to our attitude can change the whole perspective and even change the reality of the actual events that occur in our lives. A seemingly difficult problem could be the biggest blessing in one's life; it's all a matter of the right attitude.

יום טובה משכח יום רעה **A good day makes one forget a bad day**

יום רעה משכח יום טובה **A bad day makes one forget a good day**

This quote from Chapter 1 of תנא דבי אליהו Tana Devei Eliyahu written 2000 years ago, explains that all one needs is one good day and all the bad days will be forgotten. So work on making a good day; today should be the first day of the rest of your life.

### One Mind Only Processes One Mood at one Time

### Either Happiness or Sadness

According to the famous scientist Albert Einstein in his theory of relativity of space "Two things cannot occupy the same space". A person is either happy or sad, it is impossible for a person to be happy and sad at the same time! Freewill choice gives us the opportunity to choose either to be happy or sad. This is the great choice of life to be creatively loving and constructive OR hatefully, sad and destructive.

Its so simple, just choose a life of happiness and positive thinking then by the spiritual law of Tana Devei Eliyahu תנא דבי אליהו and more scientific law of Albert Einstein, will mean that sadness cannot find any room in one's mind, thoughts and soul. Once the focus of one's mind and thoughts is pointed, concentrating on and constantly aware to think of positive and happy thoughts then all the negative thoughts will be forgotten instantaneously. The challenge is to stay POSITIVE, and never allow in any negative or destructive emotions or other people with their emotional negative baggage.

**Simple Advice to Help One Stay Positive**

Realize that you have more than 5 mins to live, thank GOD for the gift of life and use your time actively, lovingly and constructively.

**Simple Guidelines and Advice to Help One Stay Positive**

**1. Prepare for a positive day the evening before and a have good nights sleep**

יומם יצוה ה חסדו ובלילה שירה עמי

Talmud Avoda Zora 3b גמרא עבודה זרה ג

In order to have a wonderful successful day it is vital that one prepares the evening before. The spiritual law is that the night is the beginning of each day. Sunset of each day is the beginning of the next day. How a person starts the day is how the remainder of the day will be. So if you want a good day, make sure that you start the preparations from the sunset the night before, as each day starts spiritually from the sunset and evening before the day.

This has important significance to one who watches TV in the evening, seeing a sad, depressing, violence or anything hateful, or even just watching anything unreal and of no actual consequence to real people living in a real world; all such negative influences will affect a person the following day.

Therefore, be careful what one does in the evening, use the peaceful evenings to think and talk, constructive, loving, happy and funny things. If one does want to watch TV or use internet only watch something funny, comedic and positively uplifting or spiritual enlightening. Don't watch the news - as most news reported is depressing and sad! Listen to romantic or classical music will put a person in a pleasant mood.

Most importantly, spend some quality time, either writing a diary or talking to oneself about one's objectives in life. Spend 10 mins before going to sleep praying. Think about the past day and one's wishes for the next day, think positively, that tomorrow will be a lovely day. If one is stuck in an unpleasant situation then repeat positively before going to sleep:-

## GOD will make a way - where there seems to be no way

A stage of spiritual maturity of living life in this physical world is to admit that a person cannot work everything out and that one needs Divine help. Admitting this truth and saying "GOD, please make a way for me where there seems to be no way", has an amazing affect on one's soul; and it works!

## 2. Think Loving Thoughts and use Positively Good Words

The key to open up the future of happiness, success and purposeful contentment in life is to learn to LOVE life. Use one's thoughts to think loving thoughts. This is not easy, especially if one has lived a spiritually void and destructive life until now. The solution is to talk to your mind with positive words.

## Talk with Calmness and Dignity

This means learning to talk differently. All aggressive, destructively critical and spiritually-void people talk without thinking, they are also talk with aggression, force and exceedingly loud. If you notice the way you talk when you are with them, is in the same way as they talk, then they are affecting your soul, then you must disconnect from communicating with them.

Whereas, people whom are spiritually enlightened always think about every single word they say, they talk eloquently, calmly and softly spoken. Their speech is always elegantly refined. Likewise if in their company you are sensitive to talk eloquently then they will bring the best out in you, and they are of tremendous good influence to you.

Good people always see goodness in everything, and always have a vocabulary of lovely words like:- "tranquility", "lovely", "delightful", "peaceful", "harmony", "excellent" etc., all their loved one's, friends and children will have nicknames of affection like "Sweettie" , "Honey" etc., A good person always exudes an energy of love and kindness for everyone and everything, and will always see the positive and goodness, and one will hear the love, calmness and eloquent dignity in the power of their speech.

Change one's vocabulary and speech, to use good words that contain positive energy. Never complain or use poor language or words that imply sadness or negativity, then within 3 days of constantly being aware of one's speech will change one's life positively for the better.

Automatically, as one changes one's speech, all the people in one's life who are negative and depressing suddenly disappear, this is because the essence of one's spiritual soul is contained with one's speech, they feel the need to disconnect with you as the quality of your soul has changed, it will seem to them like you are talking a foreign language, as the language of your soul has changed. New doors open in one's life and helpful positive, loving, genuine, trustworthy, kind and loving friends are attracted into one's life.

## 3. Focus Your Thoughts on Goodness and Happiness

Focus on something you really love to do, and have done in the past. Then reenergize your soul from the happy energy of that time in your life. Remind yourself of something that happened to you in your life that was really funny, happy, and magically amazing.

Using the principle יום טובה משכח יום רעה "A good day makes one forget a bad day" then use one's mind to concentrate in only having a happy day with happy thoughts. Block out and refuse to connect with anything or anyone who will and has ever spoilt one's good mood.

## Think of the Really Happy Moments in Ones Life

Every single person has had really happy moments in life. Think carefully, try and relive in one's memory those really happy occasions. There are moments in everyone's life, which one laughed so much that one can never forget those moments. Without these special moments, life would have been really depressingly sad.

Concentrate one's thoughts on those really happy moments, laugh and giggle at the thoughts and events that happened. Then keep thinking about those happy and funny times throughout the day, you will see after a few days of thinking and reliving the happiness, one will start to feel magnetic to an new aliveness of happiness.

Everyone who is happy with life exudes a loving feeling, a special radiant glow of aliveness, and where there is love and happiness, there is a potential basis of contentment in life. With this sincere love of life comes a thanks and appreciation of the gift of life, this energy of inner happiness in one's mind and thoughts creates more energy to make one magnetic for even more happiness and good fortune.

It is a rule of life that happy things happen to intrinsically happy people, sadness happens to intrinsically sad people. And always remember "Everything that happens - happens for our good".

## 4 Become Part of Creation

The main reason why people feel depressed, sad and worthless is because they are selfish. They have not changed from the childhood stage to adulthood stage of life (please read the chapter on "Stages of Change in Life"), where a child transforms from taking to becoming a creative adult that gives and creates life.

Marriage and sexual intimacy is for the purpose of creating loving energy and having children. An adult has only truly matured from a child into an adult when one's nature has changed from being a taker into one of a creator and giver of loving energy.

### Depression is the First Stage of Death

Depression is a feeling of disconnection with life energy; with symptoms of hatred, self abuse, sadness, selfishness, lies, deceit and jealousy. The only way for depressed people to survive is to drain and make other people feel sad and depressed too

However, the remedy to stop depression is to choose to live life and become part of creation, doing anything creative makes one part of the creative life-cycle on earth. Join the cycle of creation start by "Gardening" - plant seeds, nurture plants.

Simple formula to be a part of creation, plant seeds, nurture growing plants, even some simple action like watering plants is an act of creation. If you live in a city apartment, get a flowering window box, buy a plant for your workplace - desk etc., anything that is a living entity has life energy, and becoming part of sustaining the life energy makes you a part of creation.

Do absolutely anything creative; building, drawing, painting, calligraphy - writing, embroidery, knitting, helping feed the homeless, any action that puts a person in the constructive creative life cycle has the power to change one's soul.

This includes one's personal love relationships, if one needs to changes one's love life to stop having self destructive, wasteful, selfish relationships for sexual pleasures and start to recognize the reason for sexual love is to be constructively loving and create a child.

## Spiritual Creative love

In the same way that the thought energy is the most pure of spiritual energy we can create in this physical world with our physical mind, body and spiritual soul. The highest level of love energy is that of spiritual love. This connects the physical body and spiritual soul world, the love of GOD, and our sincere thanks for the gift of life is of course the highest connection. However, the connection of our loved one's whom have passed over to spirit world and ourselves has an immense power of love. And where there is love, there is life and happiness.

Think of someone you loved and someone who loved you who has died. Bring back the happy memories and connect spiritually with loving and happy feelings.

## Use your mind wisely – it's the most powerful part of you

Will you be able to say in a few weeks time that this moment today changed your life, because you changed to think positive by using your mind and soul to your maximum potential?

If so then today is the first day of the rest of your life, then when you least expect it, something great will come along to change your life making it even more purposeful, with an aliveness, vitality and a higher sense of spiritual purpose in life.

Something even greater will happen for you that you never even planned. This is a Divine spiritual blessing that is given to the truly transformed and enlightened person.

The beginning to a new changed life pathway is, by living THIS moment in the present to one's maximum potential with positive thinking. Then automatically the next moment will also be lived to fullest potential, and then the remainder of one's life in positive thinking and happiness.

# Chapter 15

## Using the Energy of the Place
## Where one Lives, Works and Sleeps

### The physical place where we live has an influence on our soul

In understanding the concept of change and correcting our lives, there is a need to change the physical space that a person lives, sleeps and work in. Our physical environment has an affect on our soul. Hence if we feel uncomfortable and unsettled with ourselves, this will be reflected in the home where we live. Take a look at a one's home it is a reflection of one's soul. Is it neat tidy and respectful or a confused cluttered mess?

Spiritually we know there is a constant interaction of energy with everything we see and experience physically with our spiritual soul; hence the good and positive energizing feeling of being in a holy peaceful and loving place, conversely being stuck in a traffic jam in a filthy and polluted city has an energizing or draining effect on our soul.

## A Clean Home = Clean Soul

Ones space is a reflection of one's character; a clean home reflects cleanliness in one's soul. Conversely by having a good physical clear out of all rubbish and useless items and items that represent one's past, this will also reflect in one's soul as a corresponding spiritual clear will start to transform your soul, out with all the old in with the new. Ones life can only receive something new once something old has left.

## Cleanliness and the "Clear Out"

The official clear out; simply tidy up and THROW OUT any rubbish; anything that you don't use, have never used and will never use, there is no need to hold onto anything useless.

Anything and everything that is unfinished, unused, unresolved, useless and disorganized no longer have any right to be in your home, so get rid of them immediately. Each of these items are creating stagnation, draining energy in your space, in your mind and in your life.

How do you know if it's useless rubbish that is causing a blockage in your life? Ask yourself these three questions: - Do I love it? Do I need it this week? Is it useful? If you can answer "yes" to any of these questions, keep the item in question; if "no" throw it away immediately.

One will feel an amazing inner feeling, as you clear out the past. As you do this, you will immediately feel a change, its quite an overwhelmingly and amazing experience, one of the most enjoyable parts of changing because you will really feel it as you have a massive clear-out of the past . As you also clearing out physically you have in your mind that you are also clearing our spiritually.

Things that are loved, used and appreciated have strong, vibrant energy around them. When we surround ourselves with things we love, things that have vibrant energy we have clarity and focus in our lives. When we are surrounded with things that hold negative memories, things that are no longer useful, things we don't love, we lack focus and direction.

As you do this, you will immediately feel a change, its quite an overwhelmingly and amazing experience, one of the most enjoyable parts of changing because you will really feel it as you have a massive clear-out of the past . As you also clearing out physically you have in your mind that you are also clearing our spiritually.

This also applies to your office desk, how much junk is hidden in the drawers, items you keep as a "maybe" you will need them, when in fact you will never need them. If you are still living in the past by holding onto papers dated years ago, this will prevent you from moving onto your future.

**After a Break-Up of a Bad Relationship or Divorce have a "Clear Out"**

After a divorce to disconnect with that relationship, clear everything out that reminds you of that relationship, disconnect completely. It will help you move on to the future, and bring someone more suitable into your life. Get rid of all the photos of the past love, holding onto anything from that ex-lover will keep a person in the past and prevent one moving onto the future, holding onto anything negative from the past will also interfere with any new energy, love or relationship coming into one's life.

How many times when the new love comes and sees something from an "ex-lover", it creates tension and disturbs the new relationship; so clear out the past NOW.

**The Most Important Rule is Do it now! Don't be lazy!**

If you want to change and improve your life both physically and spiritually, don't waste anymore time - get on with it NOW. Stop reading this book and do it NOW! It's far more important to get rid of one useless item from one past than to read this book!

**2. Dead space, filth and dirt attracts death**

If there is a corner in your home that you use for storing rubbish or a room / space that you do not use, this reflects in your character that you are not utilizing part of your soul. DEAD SPACE is the cause of stagnation in one's life and attracts more useless rubbish. The recipe to life is to utilize your fullest potential every facet and part of your soul, having the potential gift to help others and not using them is a form of abuse and death.

If you have a room or space that you never use, try rearranging your furniture so that the space becomes a used space with life energy. Even place a vase of flowers in that space to give it energy and life.

## Fresh Air

Always give the dead space fresh air regularly, open the windows and allow air to circulate, this will also bring a life energy. Hence the custom after someone has died, at the end of the 7 days of mourning at the "Shiva House", the custom is to open all the windows and doors for the day to allow in new life energy.

## 3. The Importance of a Healthy Energizing Pure Sleep    פנו לכם צפונה

"Turn and face north" Deuteronomy chapter 2 verse 3, when Moses instructed the Jewish people to be more spiritually minded he told them to face NORTH. The famous Kli Yakar כלי יקר explains that north is the most spiritual direction, the north reflects a direction of quiet inner introspection and spiritual growth.

## Ones Sleeping Direction

A healthy and strengthening sleep this gives your body and soul the re-charge it needs to live. The sleep you have is the one of the single most important times of the day.

So let us look at the first and foremost, imagine getting in the back seat to drive a car , you would first have to climb over the seats with difficulty to get into the drivers seat .

Have you ever woken up in the morning and simply feel so drained and tired that it takes an hour before you feel you have actually arrived inside your body?

During sleep, your soul essence leaves your body, by sleeping in the most harmonious place and direction; your soul will arrive back in your body with peace and at ease.

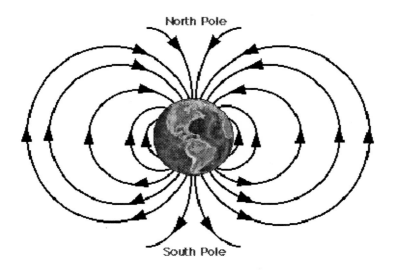

North Pole

South Pole

## A Compass Always Points North

The earth consists of electromagnetic energy fields; for those of you whom are non-scientifically minded, there are lines of energy going from the South Pole to the North Pole. Wherever you are in the world with a compass, it always points to North, that's because a compass needle goes to the place it is at ease with itself and that is to point NORTH. Even if you forced the compass needle to face east, it would still point NORTH.

Similarly everything on planet earth, every cell in our body consists of energy, and we are all as sensitive like a compass to directions. Hence there are two ideal directions for a good sleep, and that is EITHER facing NORTH or Facing SOUTH. Any slight alteration crosses energy fields, may arise in an unsettled sleep.

### Sleeping North

Sleeping North means your head is North and your feet South. This is always the best place for small children and old people, or anyone needing a really quiet life, after operation or trauma, after a divorce or break up when you need the traditional three months space alone, try sleeping North especially when you need a resting peaceful time in your life; time on your own, to think and change as we all know the best spiritual changes occur in the most quiet times of your life.

## Sleeping South

Sleeping South, means your head is South and feet pointing North. This direction of sleep means that your body is in harmony with the earth's electromagnetic energy fields, and flowing in the same way from South to North Pole, from your head to your feet. This will give you a strong sleep and wake up feeling alive and vibrant. I recommend this for everyone as the best way to sleep.

## Sleeping East

Sleeping East cuts across the magnetic energy fields and is in harmony with the suns energy rising from the east, if you are looking for new fresh start, a new outlook on life, then this direction will give you the aliveness, motivation and new start energy you need.

Depending on the time of the year, when you want your new energy boost in harmony with the rising sun, may make a difference to whether sleeping East is indeed North East of South East, that is to say point your head in the direction of sunrise.

## Working out the best direction

Only you will know the best direction, I f you are waking up in the morning feeling tired and heavy and as though you have got in the "back seat of the car" and you need time to climb into your body and take control, this implies you are sleeping in the wrong direction.

## Strongest Position

Arrange your bed or desk so you are supported by a wall behind you and you face into the room or office. Your position should provide a full view of the room and the door into the room. When your view is expansive, so are your opportunities. Likewise, sitting in a swivel chair, makes you flexible and open to all kinds of opportunities.

Place something inspiring in front of you, as you gaze out from your bed or desk. Fresh flowers are always highly recommended; especially those will beautiful and powerful scent, like rose and lilies. You are profoundly affected by the environment around you; take the time to make it an environment you want to be in and the best for your soul.

# Chapter 16

## Understanding the Importance of Ones Physical Good Health & Diet

### 1. Understanding the Physical body is a Reflection of Ones Soul

אין חוט של מחט נוגע בך ...
אלא אם כן נגזר עליך מלמעלה

Not even a pin prick can touch or harm a person, unless it is decreed upon in spirit world.

The fundamental basis of understanding and ability to heal is to accept the principal belief that absolutely NOTHING happens in this life by chance or accident. Every single event that occurs in our lives happens for a reason, and in accordance with spiritual law.

With this knowledge that EVERYTHING happens for a specific purpose and our soul is on a journey through this physical life as a transition from the spirit world from where we came to the spirit world we are going to, we start to live life a continuous journey for our soul, and therefore there is NO SUCH thing as TERMINAL for spiritually awakened. The expression "terminal" only exists to people who do not believe in a soul hence do not believe there is a spiritual existence after this physical life.

This makes the possibility to heal any illness, an intrinsic belief for anyone and everyone, even someone suffering from a so called "terminal" illness by the medical profession; spiritually awakened people throughout the whole world know that there is no such thing as terminal!

Ask anyone who has been diagnosed with cancer, after the initial period of panic and devastation, which is perfectly normal, (so don't think one is any less a person because of these feelings of fear and panic). The next stage is to use one's strength of determination, character and one's soul to LISTEN to one's inner spiritual belief that every problem has a solution, and life is continuous as the soul is everlastingly continuous, hence if it destiny one will be healed.

In our generation, we have all seen and know of thousands of people who have been cured from cancer, because they became spiritually aware of their soul, recognizing that the illness is just a physical sign to make them aware that their soul needs healing . Thereby changing one's "attitude" to life, changing one's whole personality to becoming genuinely loving, kind, calmer and accepting of life, with not even a single hateful, bitter, resentful or jealous thought in one's body.

When we say spiritual aware - we must stress that we do not mean the person has become a religious fanatic! As we all know almost all religions are man-made laws, and have been the root cause of more death hatred and misery in the world than any illness. What is meant by "spiritually aware", applies to every human on our planet - it is that one has connected with true spirituality, love of our CREATOR, love of mankind, and love of every moment of life. LOVE gives life and vitality to live.

**The Spiritual Law of the Physical Body Reflects the Soul**

Everything that occurs in this world occurs in pairs, for example, every part of our body comes in "twos", and similarly every living entity in this world comes in a pair - male and female. Likewise every action and happening that occurs in this world has an exact identity in spirit world. If something happens here in our physical world then there is a corresponding energy in the spiritual world.

This is the reason why earthquakes, floods, volcano eruptions on earth have been symbolic of actual energies in spirit world. These are catastrophic signs that "the earth" – "spirit world" is not happy with our behaviour, it is a sign from heaven, a time for each person and society to change.

## Reading the Signs from the Physical body

The right side reflects logic, the left side reflects emotions, for example, if one has an earache in the right ear, it means that one is not listening to logic and common-sense. If one has an earache in the left ear, then one is not listening to one's emotions.

When a specific part of our body is not working, this is a sign that we are NOT using that part of body properly, as it is supposed to be used. If one has broken one's right leg, this means that one's logic was wrong and leading a person in the wrong direction. If it was the left leg, then one's emotions are leading one in the wrong direction.

The Book of Healing & Corrections "Sefer Tikunim" explains every part of one's body and will be translated and published in English by ourselves during summer 2006, on the website www.tikunim.com.

## The Major Cause of Ill Health

Spiritually, the major cause of ill health is when a person lives a life disconnected spiritually; "spiritually connected" means being filled with a Godly spiritual loving energy all the time, and recognizing the existences of a soul that is continually connected to the eternal Divine spiritual world. Wherever there is Gods' love and energy, there is life, hope, faith and true happiness.

## 2 Healing the Body "Naturally"

In recognizing that our body is a reflection of our spiritual soul, healing the body "naturally" means, finding the root cause spiritually and healing the SOUL.

שׁוֹמֵר פִּיו וּלְשׁוֹנוֹ ... שׁוֹמֵר מִצָּרוֹת נַפְשׁוֹ

"Guarding one's mouth and one's speech will protect one's soul from pain and troubles". The inherent power of speech has the potential to bring life or death, happiness or sadness, good health or ill health. The first stage of good health is to use the power of one's speech wisely.

**Food & Digestion**

תחילת חולי הגוף בחולי מעיים

**The beginning of all bodily illnesses begins with illnesses in the stomach - digestion**

The famous Jewish rabbi known as Rambam in his book Hilchos Daos הלכות דעות of Mishne Torah advises the best way to remain healthy is to make sure that one's complete digestive system is given a "clear out" once every 2 to 4 weeks .

It is accepted in the knowledgeable medical profession today, that in everyone's body contains cancerous cells, one of purposes of the digestive system is to clear these cells out of the body. The stomach - intestines, as food travels through the intestines, the body absorbs the good energy of the food, whilst the cancerous cells all taken the opposite way and out of the body in the faeces - excrement. If one's intestines are not cleared regularly and fully flushed out, then these harmful cells remain trapped. Doctors are now proving how right the RAMBAM is in advising a thorough regular bodily cleansing "clear-out"!

## Prune Juice - Natures Best Natural Laxative

Flushing one's system out completely using nature's best natural laxative Prune Juice is wonderfully refreshing and healing for everyone. A glass-full 200ml is normally adequate, although for an average size person and for the first time "clear-out" should take up to 400ml of prune juice, and between 3 and 6 hours it will rocket through your body!

The feeling as this is happening is quite remarkable and almost magical, as in the same way physically deadly cells are being cleared-out of the body, so too one feels a spiritually refreshed and cleansed.

On the day of clearing one's system, drink water, no food, and allow one's digestive system to have a rest. Try it and see, one actually feels amazingly refreshed, almost like a new born baby. Then one should start food intake by having a glass of milk.

## Milk - the Most Spiritually Energizing Drink

Milk is a product connected with the life cycle of reproduction; only after a cow has given birth do the hormones and energy of the cow produce milk. Drinking milk throughout all generations has been associated with receiving the energy of growth. In the same way it has energy of physical growth it contains the energy of spiritual growth. Hence all the references in the bible to "a land flowing of milk and honey"; a sign of physical and spiritual, wealth, good health, happiness and prosperity.

## Honey – A Gift from All the Combined-Forces of "Nature"

"A land flowing of milk and honey"; honey is known as an exceedingly spiritual food, this is because every part of creation has worked together to produce Honey. Firstly the sun shines and rain waters the plants and flowers to grow. Then in the life cycle of plants, they produce nectar, which attracts the bees to pollinate and reproduce the plant by rubbing the pollen it has picked up from many plants it has visited. This pollination provides the plant with the ability to reproduce seeds and continue the cycle of life, whilst the bee takes the nectar and produces honey. The making of HONEY by the nectar in the plants and the bees is considered a spiritual gift to humans.

Tasting Honey and recognizing where it has come from, that all the collective energies of different parts of creation, which have worked together to produce HONEY, will give a person a very spiritual energy.

There are many other foods that should be eaten such as Apples; "An apple a day - keeps the doctor away", and of course there are many good spiritual books with explanations that should be read on this subject such as Sefer Refuah – The Book of Healing and Sefer Chidushim (see www.chidushim.com ).

## Cooking and preparing your food with LOVE

Better to eat food made by a automated machine than by a person with hateful energy, food infected with hate is like a poisonous cancer to the body .The divine energy in this world is LOVE, it is the creative energy. Every person should learn to cook with love and enjoyment. Food and eating are the wonderful pleasures that we can enjoy every day of our lives, so learn to LOVE cooking with love and feeding your soul.

## The Strength & Power of Prayer to heal

The power of speech in prayer is the most powerful way to heal one's spiritual soul. Every human has the spiritual potential to pray and have their prayers answered. There is no distinction in religion or beliefs, in race or age. Every human who has the power of speech, has the power to pray, and definitely have one's prayers answered through the help of their own unique Guardian Angels whose sole purpose is to listen to one's prayers and help.

## Holding the Hand of a Sick Person

As we explained in the chapter on Palmistry, the energy of one's soul is contained in the palms of one's hand. In shaking hands or holding hands, this enables transference of energy between the souls. Hence spiritual healers always made a special point to shake hands with sick people.

Try and see for yourself, when you go to hospital, old age home or to visit a friend / family, who are sick at home, simply hold hands. The sick person will feel the spiritual and physical energy transfer and actually start to feel healthier, simply by holding hands.

The reason is simple, the healthy person is wholesome both physically and spiritually, a sign that the soul is directly linked spiritually to spirit world. Whilst holding hands the healthy person acts as a medium to bring down and channel spiritual energy to heal the person's soul.

## 3 Sexual Good Health for Our Generation

In this section we shall indicate areas that our generation is neglecting compared with previous generations, we believe to be primarily due to lack of education.

### חיבור ונישוק - "Making Love"

The traditional Hebrew term for making love is חיבור ונישוק , meaning "connection and kissing". This is to stress that importance of good sexual behaviour following a spiritual way of life is to connect one's body & soul together. Many people say, what one does in bed is one's own choice; however, the wrong sexual behaviour does have an affect on one's soul, conversely following the correct sexual way enhances a loving relationship, making it long lasting and stable with a physical and spiritual vitality.

### The levels of the soul contained in the physical body

1. Nefesh (Earthly soul) נפש , the most physical of spiritual energy, opens and connects through the sexual organs, a mans penis inside a woman's vagina.

2. Ruach (Spirit of Soul through breathe) רוח , the spiritual energy contained in the breathe of life . Our speech is a reflection of our Spirit of "Ruach". Kissing with one's lips and mouth connects the two spirits of people.

3. Neshama (Pure Spiritual Soul) נשמה , all our minds higher thoughts and energies we use with concentration . The heightened energized state of sexual orgasm connects one's Neshama - soul at the highest level.

### The spiritually correct way for "making love"

Simple ! A man on top of a woman facing each other, lying down in a bed, with his erect penis inside a woman's vagina ONLY .

## Connecting all levels of the soul.

Whilst making love, moving in and out inside the vagina, the man and the woman, kiss each other to connect the breath of life the "Ruach – Spirit" of the souls with their mouths, whilst their sexual organs are connecting their bodies as a wholesome body. As both come to heightened energy of orgasm then their souls "Neshoma" unites on the highest level possible physically and spiritually, which is the recipe for making love and for bringing down a new spirit soul of a child.

According to the ARI and Reb Chaim Vital, every time one makes love correctly an angel is created, even if a child is not conceived, to enhance their lives spiritually and physically successfully with good fortune.

Many people will tell, that they have amazing good fortune Mazal & success, especially when they "make love" properly the night before. A sign that a person is not acting correctly is that they have failure in their life, as a sign they are "wasting" or destroying a creative energy from their destructive wasteful acts of sexual behaviour.

Staying inside a woman and connecting sexually for as long as possible, both physically and spiritually is the purpose of the act of making love. Staying inside and moving slowly with LOVE, and NOT in a hurried state of aggression and panic, but with good thoughts and self- control will connect the two souls together with a divine creative love energy .

## The Wrong Wasteful Ways "Short circuits" all the levels of the soul

The simple way to correct any wrong behaviour from the past is to STOP, immediately stopping the wrong acts cleanses and heals the soul. In our generation, there have been many instances of wrong behaviour, which all the spiritual teachers find unbelievable. Therefore, we make mention of these wrongs and explain spiritually the damage to the soul.

For a woman to touch a penis, with her hand or with her mouth will damage BOTH their souls. As spiritually this act connects the Spirit "breath" of one person with the Animal Nefesh of another, this lowers the level of the Spirit Ruach to a Animal Nefesh.

דין עלך עשרה יוחסין אף מי שיש לו ואינה שריה אצלו לא ילמד סופרים: ר יהודה אומר לא ירעה מי: תניא אמרו לו לרבי יהודה לא נחשדו ישראל על משכב זכר ולא על הבהמה: מתני כל ישעסקו עם הנשים לא יתיחד עם הנשים ולא ילמד אדם את בנו אומנות הנשים רבי מאיר אומר לעולם ילמד אדם את בנו אומנות נקיה וקלה ויתפלל למי שהעושר ותנכסים שלו שאין אומנות שאין בה עניות ועשירות שלא עניות מן האומנות ולא עשירות מן האומנות אלא הכל לפי זכותו רבי שמעון בן אלעזר אומ

For anyone to have "anal sex" like homosexuals, which the Talmud in Kiddushin 82a (the text is reproduced above) explains that truly human spiritual souls will never have, implying that anyone who acts homosexually is NOT a human soul. The very next section of the Talmud talks about success in life, connecting the fact that when one behaves morally and sexually correct one has true and lasting success.

The act of "anal sex" means, that the mans physical sexual organ representing the souls energy of creation and life is connecting with the most destructive energy a human can create - excrement, disgusting and vile deadly energy.

The act of "anal" activity connects the soul "Nefesh" directly with DEATH. Once a person has been in direct contact with this death energy, their soul level of NEFESH is dead and disconnected spiritually, and anyone they connect with, will kill with their "death" energy. Accordingly, the biblical story of "Sodom and Gomorra" explains that these cities were destroyed as it lacked any LIFE energy.

"Coming outside" to avoid pregnancy or wearing a condom or any other perversion of women touching genitals of the man will corrupt and short circuit the soul. This is because at the moment of heightened state of orgasm the soul is trying to make a strong connection, if there is a blockage by way of condom, or the penis is removed to disconnect, the spiritual energy of their souls have no way of connecting, so it actually creates a destructive energy.

Similarly wasting "seed" in masturbation; this act brings one's soul to heightened level of spiritual consciousness and orgasm, but has no one to connect the sexual spiritual energy, and is wasted. The ARI and Reb Chaim Vital, quote the ZOHAR that the destructive energy created in masturbation, causes a destructive energy (actually a destructive angel is created) that hangs around a person for a whole day until sunset the following day.

The ספר קב הישר Sefer Kav HaYosher - explains that a woman's body a certain times, becomes hot and sexually aroused, and can even "let themselves go" - masturbate in public places. According to ספר קב הישר Sefer Kav HaYosher, this releases a spiritual energy but it also affects sensitive people in the vicinity. The book asks and pleads with women to control themselves especially in public places.

Understanding that women have sexual needs and desires, more than men, as their sexual desires are given by GOD in order to help continue the human race, desiring children is a GOD-given natural gift for all normal women. This is the way that GOD made and has blessed the woman's body, but asks women to restrain themselves in public places, and use this excitable energy to either focus in praying, loving and desiring their true soulmate or if women really need to "let themselves go" to release their inner tension and masturbate, then only in private and never in public amongst people .

The relationship, even if it is a destined soulmate can be ruined, by one act of sexual degradation. Disease ...the name itself means DIS.... EASE, reflects that a person is not at ease with themselves, their souls are not at peace and will never be a peace ... if it is diseased. When the act of making love is done correctly it brings pleasure and life energy to both the man and the woman.

As everyone is aware there are two ways of doing everything in life, the correct way and incorrect way, making love with aggression and with an energy to satisfy an animal instinct is NOT the correct way . Making love, out of a desire of peace, love, dignity, serenity and a desire to connect one's souls together in unity is the absolute correct way.

The highest form of creative activity of the human being is making love between a man and a woman, which creates a spiritual energy that brings then closer to GOD and Spirit world. The act of making love will leave one's soul feeling alive with spiritual energy having just connected with GODLY loving energy.

### The Women's body is a sacred temple of the "cycle of life"

The physical body of a woman is the symbol of creative life on earth. Together with the man, a woman's body becomes the home of a growing baby / child during pregnancy. The marvelous miracle of creation of a new born life, takes place in the woman's body.

### Menstruation - Women's Period

The cycle of life on earth, birth and death, occurs monthly within a women's body. The potential to create life is a monthly potential. Once the opportunity is missed, then a form of "death" occurs, in the form bleeding. It is known throughout the world, that the just before the time of bleeding a woman becomes exceedingly sensitive and emotional. This is her soul sensing this level of "death" which is about to arrive. Depending on the attitude of mind of the woman, she will handle the period in much the same way as handling a "death".

Therefore according to both Jewish tradition and sacred Kabbalistic knowledge and understanding, it is forbidden for men and women to have sexual relations whilst a woman is "bleeding" during the monthly menstrual cycle, which normally lasts at least 5 days .

The reason is simple, a woman represents LIFE, the reason for sexual relations is to create life, whilst the menstruation - bleeding is occurring, this is symbolic of DEATH. Therefore LIFE and DEATH must be kept separated. It is a fact of life, that ALL marriage problems, arguments and break-downs in communication, occur during this sensitive period of Menstruation.

Therefore spiritually and common sense decency, it is so important that both men and women realize the "period" time must be treated with mutual respect for the cycle of life. This is the reason why all Jewish spiritual laws and Kabbalistic traditions require men and women to abstain from sexual relations during this "bleeding period"

The quality of one's loving relationship, quality of one's life both physically and spiritually is enhanced when one keeps the sanctity and purity of abstinence of sexual relations during the period. According to Reb Chaim Vital, the famous kabbalist, it is also a blessing that one's children, especially the quality of the SOUL of one's children is so much more pure and blessed with an intrinsic purity, when the parents keep "family purity". It is accepted that one's eye colour is a reflection of the quality and purity of one's soul, and influenced by the purity of sexual relationship of one's parents.

## Keeping Your Hands Clean

Ones hands contain the energy of your soul, both imprinted on it in the form of lines, but also in the energy of your hands is the energy of your soul. So be careful for physical and spiritual cleanliness and good health to always keep one's hands clean.

## Guard Your Eyes

Your eyes are the windows of your soul, so in the interest and good health of protecting your soul BE CAREFUL WHAT YOU LOOK AT. Headaches are "Spiritual Attacks" that one has been attacked through seeing something through one's physical and spiritual eyes.

## Respecting Your Feet

The feet represent the foundations of your physical body; there is a tremendously strong spiritual energy in your feet. Acupuncturists and alternative medicine have recognized the power of spiritual and nerve energy within a person's foot. There are also spiritual lines on one's feet - just like the lines on one's hand.

The feet reflect the foundation of one's body and soul, take a look at your feet, what condition are they in?

The remedy is simple; wash them at least TWICE a day in the morning and evening. If one has dry skin, then use natural cocoa butter to rub into your feet. Give your feet fresh air - never wear socks in bed (unless you're in really freezing conditions in the North Pole or camping in Siberia!).

Make sure that you always have the most comfortable pair of shoes. Never wear a pair of shoes because they "look good" to others, but hurt your feet! Such a silly attitude - reflects one's character.

## "The 5 minute rule" from Sefer Shinuyim

The Book of Changes "Sefer Shinuyim" explains that if you had just 5 minutes left to live, what would you do in the last 5 minutes of life, and how would you like to be remembered?" Start behaving and treating one's body with dignity, sanctity as if you have just 5 minutes to live, this will then stop a person from doing silly things and living a wasteful futile life.

Once a person starts to cherish the gift of life as if every 5 mins are one's last 5 mins, then one's whole body will start to feel better as one's soul will become at peace within one's physical body with a peace of mind and good health.

# Chapter 17

## Unblocking one's life by saying "Thank You GOD"

The continuous flow of life's energy is dependant on the recognition and saying the simple words "THANK YOU". By saying "thank you" for anything and everything that is in one's life, is a sign of appreciation to the "benefactor", that one has received the energy of life and wishes to continue the flow.

It is the best way to release any awkward situation and difficulties one has, by genuinely coming to the level of appreciation for everything in one's life is the best way to show one is now ready to "move on" to the next stage of life. Likewise the best way to stay attached to a situation, person or place is by complaining.

By giving thanks for every situation and seeing the good in everything, this will reflect spiritually in one's soul is now learning and progressing forward in life.

### 1. The First Impression

What are the first words and questions new acquaintance asks you? How did you react to your first encounter with that new person in your life? These aspects identifies the character of the person and of your relationship with them. Either they will be a "giver", "taker", user or abuser, honest or deceitful, constructive or destructive, happy or sad, good or bad or someone your can create life energy with.

When one meets someone new, the first words they ever say, identifies their character to you. Whatever the first impression is to you, this is engrained in your mind and soul. Likewise, your first impression to others has the same affect.

Each person is identified by the words they use. People whom you meet, if the first question they ask you is work / business related, this is a reflection on their character that is what THEY are concerned with - materialism . If a person asks you about your health, welfare or something of importance then they are genuinely concerned for you, this reflects their kindness. If they are using negative words and complaining - then RUN AWAY from them, they are bad! If they are using positive constructive, loving and kind words - they are good!

**The First Date**

When dating, the questions people ask you are more important than the answers. The questions "the date" is asking are the primary concerns the person has. Do they continually want to know your financial status, career, job and materialistic ideals, or are they concerned with the charitable/voluntary work you do to help others?

**Identify them - Are they Constructive or Destructive?**

The world needs all kinds of people, and maybe a person feels good amongst materialistic and the "shallow minded people" whom live for the animalistic pleasures of today, and not thinking for a single moment in anything spiritual, that is their problem and their chosen stage of life, just beware that they don't influence you and don't you join such a shallow group of people.

For those people who are seeking and searching for a purposefully enlivened life on an enlightened pathway, then it is of vital importance to identify the characters of people one meets as soon as possible; attaching with the good and appreciative, running away & "having closure" from the troubled and complaining type.

**2. Going Around in "Circles" is a Punishment for Complaining**

The Spiritual concept that going around in circles in life is a punishment for complaining, as the rule if one doesn't stop complaining then life will give a person reasons to complain applies. Learning to break the cycle by STOP complaining, learning to appreciate life and give THANKS!

The Book of Reincarnation Sefer Gilgulim explains that all souls that have been reincarnated are here to learn the lesson to appreciate the goodness of life, and to overcome the urge of "COMPLAINING" against GOD for the life one has. The reason a person has the life one has, is in order to learn the lesson of appreciation, as it could always be far worse!

In Sefer Gilgulim, the Book of Reincarnation, these complaining souls are referred to as souls from the "wilderness דור המדבר " - complainers מתעוננים , whom GOD punished by letting them wander around in circles in the wilderness for 40 years as a punishment for complaining. This is a lesson for everyone, the punishment of feeling stagnated and wandering around in circles in life, without really accomplishing anything, identifies to one's soul an urgent need to change - only one aspect of one's life :-

## STOP COMPLAINING

This is the simple spiritual law for a successful & purposeful life of inner happiness & peace by simply "Stop complaining". Learning to be grateful and happy for everything that happens in life is one of the most important lessons in life for spiritual progress.

המבעט ביסורים ... כופלין לו

**"One who complains about problems then the problems are doubled"**

If one does NOT change, the Book תנא דבי אליהו Tana Devei Eliyahu says, "one who complains about problems then the problems are doubled". The whole purpose of pain and problems is to wake a person up SPIRITUALLY. If one has not woken up, then more pain is sent to try and wake up the person in a different way.

The real reason a person has failures in life, is to make one aware that one has a disconnection with GOD, or one is denying existence that a spiritual afterlife, as the eternal DIVINE spirit world is the only source of "life-giving" loving creative energy of this world, if one is truly connected one will feel at peace with oneself and with everything in one's life.

The reason pain occurs in life, is due to some level of a disconnection with GOD. Once the person has woken up to become loving instead of hateful, constructive instead of destructive, spiritually awakened instead of like the living "dead" spiritually, appreciative of life instead of complaining, then the purpose of pain is fulfilled and the painful lesson will be taken away.

Start thinking in terms of seeing the good in people and seeing the good in everything that happens in one's life. Look for reasons to give compliments, using kind and loving words, then one will feel attached to the unity of the world instead of being lonely selfish and detached.

When a person starts to see the good in everything that happens in life, then only good can happen, even if other people see it as "bad luck", a spiritually aware person - always sees and feels the goodness in everything that happens.

## Learning to be Appreciative and Say "THANK YOU GOD"!

God's abundant life giving energy is a flow - like a river. In the universal spirit law of flow of energy, energy MUST continue flowing, wherever there is a stagnation or blockage, inevitably means death.

One of the greatest gifts given to every living entity on this planet is the inherent feeling desire and emotion to want to give to others. When parents give love, help, support, food and clothing to their children they are overwhelmed by a sense of purpose in life. The more generous, kind and loving - the more energy and good fortune flows through and is attracted into one's life.

In exact proportion as you give thanks, joy and love - you will receive joy and sincere love, this is a spiritual law of reciprocity. Joy and true love increase in one's life as you give it, and diminishes as you try to keep it for the selfish self.

במדה שאדם מודד בה מודדין לו וכן מדה זו לכל באי עולם

"In the way a person behaves to others, so the person is treated by others", or as the famous saying "what goes around - comes around", if you are kind and generous to others, then life will be kind and generous to you, if one cheats and deceives others then one will be deceived.

## The Spiritual Law of Continuity of Flow

The spiritual law of continuity of flow of love and energy means that whatever you give to one person, never expect it back from them, the flow of love, energy and good fortune will come from somewhere else, just like a flowing river. A flow of nature means giving in one place and receiving from another.

## Learn to say "THANK YOU"

Say "Thank You" for anything and everything in your life. Just say the words "Thank you GOD" a hundred times now and see for yourself, that's right open your mouth and say the words loudly "Thank you GOD"; as you hear yourself say the words "Thank you GOD" you will immediately feel much better, like it has opened up a magical door inside your head and don't be surprised if something good happens very shortly!

These words have an affect on one's soul, and they do take away negative blockages from one's life. Just say the words "Thank you GOD" even if you don't mean it, as soon you will find reasons that you really do mean it!

## Begin to appreciate what you have and say:-

## THANK YOU !

# THANK YOU !

# THANK YOU !

# THANK YOU GOD !

Once a person has broken the cycle of complaining and bad attitude of mind, learnt to appreciate and give thanks for even the smallest of thing in life, one will feel reborn. With this new attitude to life, one will find that there will be so many wonderful changes, which will make one's life feel purposeful with an inner spiritual glow of happiness and peace of mind.

**"Footprints" by an Anonymous Author**

One night a man had a dream. He dreamed he was walking along the beach with the Lord. Across the sky flashed scenes from his life. For each scene, he noticed two sets of footprints in the sand; one belonging to him and the other to the Lord.

When the last scene of his life flashed before him, he looked back at the footprints in the sand. He noticed that many times along the path of his life there was only one set of footprints. He also noticed that it happened at the very lowest and saddest times in his life.

This really bothered him and he questioned the Lord about it. "Lord, you said that once I decided to follow you, you'd walk with me all the way. But I have noticed that during the most troublesome times in my life, there is only one set of footprints. I don't understand why when I needed you most you would leave me."

The Lord replied, "My precious child, I Love you and would never leave you. During your times of trial and suffering, when you see only one set of footprints, it was then that I carried you."

## Appreciating the Divine Help

Everyone has experienced difficulties and continues to face challenges everyday, however, once one adapts a spiritual attitude to life, learning to accept difficulties as tests of one's character, learning the lessons of one's circumstances and appreciating the gift of life, then anything else that is beyond a persons abilities to solve one can always ask in prayer from GOD and one's Guardian Angels to help.

## A Candle - the Spiritual Light of Hope

Whenever one needs to feel the energy of the eternal Divine spiritual world, simply light a candle a pray, ask GOD to make a way where there seems to be no way and always remember to thank GOD and one's Guardian Angles for everything that has happened each and every day. Then miracle shall follow miracle and wonders shall never cease, Amen.

# Chapter 18

## Spiritual Rescue Work of Lost and Earthbound Souls

Spiritual Rescue work is the name given to the process of transition of a person's soul over to spirit world once the soul has departed from the physical body.

Once a person has completed their journey in a physical body, death occurs; this simply means the SOUL leaves the physical body - entering the realm of spiritual vibration.

Initially the soul is disorientated and hovers in an earthbound state, known by the Hebrew term as wandering in Olam HaSohu - התוהו עולם , known by some people as wandering the ether, the ethereal plane, or astral plane; needing and searching for loving energy, or for someone spiritually sensitive to communicate with, with whom will give them unconditional love to feed their soul with energy, vitality and spiritual guidance.

After the initial period of a few hours after death, the soul then usually panics, especially of those souls whom had no idea that an eternal Divine Spiritual World exists or of those very religious people whom believed they would be whisked away to heaven.

The purpose of rescuers is to communicate with the earthbound soul, guide and elevate the soul onwards to the spirit world.

Everything creative and every transformation in this world is done through love and loving energy. A soul originally enters this world through the heightened state of sexual love energy of its parents, and similarly needs a strong spiritual LOVE energy to take it onward toward the divine light of spirit world, especially if the person died in a state of sadness, fear and depression that they had a futile life!

A rescuer is usually a very refined, strong and sensitive soul who is intune with eternal Divine Spirit World through their Spirit guides, helpers and Guardian angels, and is therefore able to sense the dead person's soul hovering in this earthbound state through their refined and opened 3rd spiritual eye.

A spiritual rescuer will talk to the soul, calm the panic feeling, and ask their guardian angels, spiritual guides and helpers, to take the soul on towards the Divine light. The earthbound souls, need our love and prayers of love to give their soul enough energy to elevate their soul to the Spirit world.

Normally there is someone who cries tears of love for the passed one, and there are the persons own guardian angels waiting to take the person over to spirit world. If however there is no-one, for example due to accidental premature death or the person lived a vacant spiritual life and disconnected even with their own guardian angels or simply stubbornly does not believe in GOD or spirit world - in their confusion - they are fighting their souls progression onto spirit realms and remain earthbound .

Then the soul will wander earthplane until it finds a spiritual psychically aware person whom they will make contact with, some souls can remain static and earthbound for many years.

An Original handwritten book of Sefer "Kav HaYosher" ספר קב הישר

159

Chapter 5 of Sefer "Kav HaYosher" ספר קב הישר as above in the original Hebrew, explains that the whole physical world is indeed full of lost and troubled earthbound souls, and the greatest act of kindness is for spiritually enlightened and sensitive people to RESCUE these souls and take them over to the eternal Divine Spirit world through the power of prayer.

## Method for Spiritual Rescue Work

Rescuers will send loving thoughts out to the lost soul and generate the love to help the soul over to spirit world, through their own group of spirit guides and helpers. Usually one will light a single candle as the soul is elevated to spirit world.

A spiritual rescuer closes their physical eyes and concentrates on the spiritual colours being given to them through their third eye and spiritual guardian angels, (seeing colours is accepted and usual for spiritual rescuers).

Firstly , you will see a small and intense circle of green colour usually with a black centre, if, however you see any other colour, you will have to pray & wait for and concentrate more loving energy to arrive at the green colour . Once you see this green colour, you are ready to bless this soul and ask this earthbound spirit to go with your guardian angels towards the divine white light of spirit world.

Then you will see the tunnel of white light coming closer, towards you, the green colour and any other colours will disappear and only pure white light will be infront, you will feel the peace and serenity, and nothing can harm you, although its advisable to be doing this rescue work in a quiet and peaceful place in your home without distractions.

Once the earthbound soul has departed then suddenly all the white light will disappear, and you will feel the soul has left; there will be no more panic or heavy feeling around you.

Then usually you will see the normal healing pink blue or purple colours that you usually see. You will then need a re-charge time alone, as is known "as a clearance day" where your soul replenishes, and the earthbound's remnants of heaviness are dissipated, usually done by opening the doors and windows, and allowing in fresh air is sufficient.

For those people who suffer from migraine attacks they should read the next chapter on "Healing Migraine" which explains the reason people attacked by migraine seeing aura colours is because they are actually sensing the earthbound evil spirit souls and actually doing spiritual rescue work without even knowing it!

## A different level of RESCUE WORK

It maybe that you do not see colours, but instead you just have a very strong feeling of someone's earthbound spirit presence, in which case, in exactly the same way talk to the person, as if they are really there, tell them to believe in afterlife, ask them to be calm, trusting that life has purpose and continuity, and in the process of life, now is the time they must go towards the divine white light of spirit world.

Light a candle for their soul, bless them and wish them well, if you wish - ask your spirit guides and helpers to take them along their way into spirit world towards the light. Always light a candle if you sense any panic-type feelings, most people find that lighting a candle always helps to calm the earthbound soul.

## Olam HaSohu - עוֹלם התוֹהוּ

## The Earthbound Plane known As the Astral Ethereal Plane

Is there a spirit world where the departed "souls" reside?

What happens when one dies?

Materialists, atheists and skeptics could argue that there is nothing left when we die. They believe erroneously that life is a purely biological process. For them, when the body dies, everything stops and that is the end of the personality.

For some, there is a vague uncertain something beyond the physical death. However, there are those who have no doubt that there is a life after the physical death. For them, there is a spirit world.

When someone dies, it brings home the reality that one day we will all die. One's physical body houses the spirit - soul. The body is like a garment we put on while we are alive and we discard it when we die, just like we discard our clothes.

Our soul is attached to life force of GOD, known as the spark of GOD within each of us. This life force permeates the physical, the astral, the mental, the spiritual and all levels of our soul.

When death draws close, the soul of a person gradually withdraws itself from the Physical body , and enters the ASTRAL plane - Olam HaSohu  this is not OLAM HABA - the pure spirit world , but rather an in between world . The words OLAM HASOHU - literally mean "a world of nothingness", not being physical or purely spiritual.

The spirits in the in-between-world can remain there for a very long time. Until they learn and accept within their soul, a belief in GOD and in spirit world.

The Olam HaSohu - the astral world is a "place" where beings reside when they are not in the physical. The physical world is a place where the same types of beings reside when they are not in the astral. The astral world is a complex place full of subtle entrapments just like the situations here in this physical world. In one sense it is far more deceptive than the physical dimension, in much the same way as our dreams are deceptive.

No one is wiser just because they are from the astral plane of spirit world. So do not let those from this plane of spirit world dictate to you. This is especially true when visiting mediums or clairvoyants who tell you they are contacting spirit world, when in actual fact they are receiving communication from spirits in the Olam HaSohu astral plane.

Hence the Torah - the bible telling us it is forbidden to contact the DEAD from the Olam HaSohu - astral plane, as they can be untruthful and misleading as people in this world can be! There are mischievous entities – just like in the physical world. Some will put on an air and impersonate a wise sage, even a learned Rabbi, a deceased relative or a good friend, and will try to fool you or manipulate your life.

In the Olam HaSohu - astral plane, one soon learns that everything is based on thoughts. Thus, the astral beings can use their thoughts for good or evil. They can delude themselves by creating thought forms which appear to be real and continue to live in that illusion until the bubble breaks or until they become bored and restless. Or they can utilize their thought forms to help people they damaged during their life, and hence release themselves from punishment and move on to the eternal Divine Spiritual realms of Olam Habo.

Many of us know many stories of people who died and within a few days, weeks or months of them dying their children, relatives or friends, had a change in fortune, or found their true loving soulmate. It had been blocked whilst they were alive by their negative thoughts, however in their transitional state of Olam HaSohu, in the astral plane they recognize the error of their lives, and rectify anything they can correct for the good. Once rectified their spirit is at peace and can elevate itself out of the earthbound astral plane and move to the eternal Divine spiritual realms.

## Our Lucky Generation

Through the power of readily available spiritual knowledge we live in extremely lucky and spiritually enlightened times.

In our lifetime we hope that you and many people will fulfill the prophecy of the Book of Daniel and become spiritually enlightened, acting as a piece that joins this physical world and the eternal spiritual realms of Divine Heavens. Amen.

# Chapter 19

## Spiritual Healing in a Real World –
## "Healing a Migraine"

### What is a Migraine?

A migraine or headache is a real physical pain, at the point or area of one's 3rd eye; this is the point in one's forehead between one's two physical eyes. This is coupled together with the person seeing colours and becoming very light sensitive. These colours are spiritual colours, yet they are strong and very real to the migraine sufferer, they are certainly NOT one's imagination as some skeptical Doctors believe.

Normally most people when they suffer from migraine attacks, wear dark glasses and hide away in a dark room, they feel extremely dizzy that they can only lie down and go to sleep. Most migraine sufferers are between the age of 18 and 45, specifically during the years when they are most sexually active.

"Migraine" sufferers run in the family, it is hereditary in most cases, as too are the spiritual gifts, which are associated with migraine sufferers.

### What is Migraine in Spiritual Terms?

Every physical pain is a reflection of a spiritual pain. A migraine is an attack of unpleasant or "bad spirits" on a person's soul at the sensitive spiritual entry point of one's 3rd eye.

The 3rd eye has become opened and has allowed in to one's spirit and soul, this earthbound evil spirit.

This evil earthbound spirit is full of hatred, destruction, depression and sadness, as they have lived a life devoid of love and devoid of awareness of GOD. Therefore their soul remains earthbound, as the pure spirit world does not want their soul, and they remain attached to this world, looking for good souls to steal their energy. Once they find a good soul, they drain and steal the life energy, they do this by attacking one's spirit.

### Who Suffers Migraine Headaches with Auric Colours ?

All spiritually sensitive souls suffer from migraine attacks and see auric colours. Many people think that the aura colours are bad - quite the contrary - the aura colours are in fact the amazing colours of ALL YOUR SPIRITUAL GUARDIAN ANGELS, that are trying to come close to warn you and PROTECT you, from these evil people and evil spirits.

That is why the initial reaction is to get away, go to a quiet and dark room to be away and closed from everyone. This is the instinctive protection that every sensitive soul of a migraine sufferer knows as the "Switching off" process.

### "The Migraine Attack"

Once a person has been attacked by an earthbound evil spirit, or is in danger spiritually, then one will sense the migraine headache pain, and usually start to see auric colours through one's 3rd eye.

## The Colours Indicate "Spiritual Protection"

Many people often try and ignore the pain until it becomes unbearable! Whatever the case, once a person is attacked by an earthbound spirit automatically one's spiritual Guardian Angels come close to indicate that one is under attack, they indicate their presence to you by the colours of the aura, it is usually green, purple, pink, if they are very strong guardian angels then when a person closes their eyes in a dark room a spiritual person will see an amazing blue and even a pure white light.

When a sensitive person is being attacked spiritually, even closing one's eyes and seeing these colours can make a normal person feel crazy! Don't worry! Many people experience this - and believe me you are NOT alone and you are certainly NOT going crazy!

## Healing a Migraine Spiritually

### 1. Be Alone

Instinctively all migraine sufferers do this anyway, BE ALONE, allow NOTHING or NO ONE into your life, switch all music, radios, especially TV and computer screens off, if you knew how much negative energy comes our of a TV and cathode ray old computer monitor, you would throw them away immediately!

Turn all lights off and even draw the curtains. Lay down in bed or even sit in an armchair, most people find sitting in a armchair is better than laying in a bed. Most migraine sufferers lack appetite, so the best advice is drink milk, it's natural, healthy and absorbs energy into your body, or even drink hot milk as this makes a person feel sleepy and calm.

Understand that the aura colours are NOT attacking you, they are in fact your spiritual guardian angels helping you, so look at the colours and focus on the beauty. It can be painful as the evil earthbound spirit is trying to attack you and steal energy from you.

The benefit of sleep is the fact that whilst you are sleeping your soul is being healed by the spirit world, which is also protecting you and taking the evil earthbound spirit away from you.

There is deeper meaning in sleep as this indicates you are living in the wrong place, you soul has come under attack, as you are living the wrong life in the wrong place for your body and soul. Sleep simply takes your soul to the place where your soul gets its maximum energy of vitality.

## 2. Pray

When you see the colours, pray and ask that your good angels should take the pain away from your and take this evil spirit away from you and from this world.

Take deep breathes, and feel the earthbound evil spirit going away, unlike a real person, an evil spirit consists of parts, and each part has to be eliminated. So keep on praying and taking deep breathes to help your angels get the spirit away.

After 30 mins of prayer in the peace and calmness, one will feel much better. This does not mean it's all over, but is does mean that the power of your Guardian Angels is winning over the power of this evil earthbound spirit.

## 3. Keep Closed

Whilst the spiritual healing is taking place ....keep 100% closed, don't allow anything or anyone into your life. Then try and go to sleep, for a few hours. If the colours are still there when you wake up, pray and ask for help again. Take the usual painkillers, cups of tea, glass of milk etc., but focus on the need to be closed spiritually.

Once a person understands that the migraine is indeed a spiritual attack, it actually makes it a lot easier to handle, and usually after one night it goes away. The following day, is known spiritually as - a clearance day, when the evil spirit is cleared, your guardian angels are giving you extra special energy to recharge your soul.

Slowly over the clearance day, the colours and headaches go away, in fact the headaches usually go away first, as the headache is the attack of the evil spirit, whereas the colours are the healing angels.

As every migraine sufferer experiences and knows that once the attack has finished there is a really good feeling during the clearance day, as one is being protected with extra special spiritual energy from one's Guardian Angels, together with a sense of relief that the evil earthbound spirit has gone away.

## 4. Look at the Sunshine

After the uncomfortable feelings of the earthbound evil spirit have gone away, and after a good nights sleep wake up early for the clearance day and look at the sunshine.

The healing qualities of sunlight, the eternal Divine energy sustaining the whole universe has very powerful healing affects for your soul. Sit in the sunshine for a few hours and feel the sun on your face, feel the suns energy healing and repairing your 3rd eye. The light of the sun is pure and natural healing.

Whereas, (and i have to say it), TV screens, computer monitors, even electric light bulbs, fluorescent lighting all have negative energies which can hurt your spiritual 3rd eye, this is because the electricity is emitting negative electrons in the form of light, this is the main reason why we use dark blue and yellow colours on our websites, as these colours are "soft" on one's spiritual 3rd eye!

### The Future

Now that one is aware, that migraine attacks are spiritual attacks by evil earthbound spirits, one needs to learn to be more closed and protected spiritually.

Once a person has learnt to be closed, then the frequency of attacks becomes less. These evil spirits will still try to attack such a sensitive and good soul, but once they see you are closed, they will leave you alone!

### "Destiny to Change & Move"

Migraine sufferers, due to the extreme sensitivity have an inbuilt system if self-protection, eventually and usually between the ages of 30 and 42, all migraine sufferers realize that they are living in the wrong place amongst the wrong people, as they are continually being attacked by "evil" earthbound spirit souls.

For no logical explanation, other than listening to their intuition, migraine sufferers will suddenly leave their home, life, even the people they have be friendly with, during the ages of 30 and 42, and find the ideal place for them to live both physically and spiritually. Immediately the migraine headaches and attacks will STOP!

## Cemeteries & Funerals

Cemeteries can be very peaceful and spiritually energizing places, and throughout the past 4000 thousand of years, the tradition has always been to visit the graves of holy and good people.

However, for sensitive souls - which includes migraine sufferers! This can expose one to earthbound evil spirits, So BEWARE!

This is the reason why Jewish priests Kohanim cannot go to cemeteries as they will become impure and open to be potentially attacked by earthbound evil spirits, and hence the reason that priests are allowed to visit the graves of righteous and holy rabbis.)

Likewise, hearing about someone whom has just died whoever they are, can make a person open to attack, so always be careful NOT to allow in or be OPEN to earthbound spirits .

## Migraine attacks eventually go away

As a person becomes more spiritually aware the migraine attacks will GO AWAY, as the person is becoming stronger spiritually, and one's guardian angels become more protective of you.

Remember, you are alive and the earthbound evil spirit is dead, you have the power to win together with the help of your spiritual guardian angels. After a few months you will even know instinctively how to be closed and never be drained by anything or anyone again which could cause a spiritual attack or migraine!

The pain is there as a sign to learn to be careful to keep closed in the future, once a person has learn to be closed then the pain goes away, and so too the migraines will go away forever.

## Or Admit Like I did - that you are Living the Wrong Type of Life

Personally i found that once i admitted to myself that pain had a reason and was a sign that i was living the wrong type of life, i affirmed and said:-

"ok ok ok ... enough pain ....i get the message ... and i admit i am living the wrong type of life for my soul, i admit that i am in the wrong place with the wrong partner, and amongst the wrong people, in the wrong city, so please take the pain away and get me away from these people and out of here!"

In hindsight this was the best prayer i have come up with to get rid of migraines! Then "magically" over those few months, i found myself detached from my old way of life, and from my materialistic, deceitful and draining friends, finding new friends who are creatively alive, lovely, spiritually minded and sincere, then i managed to move home within a year, and once i moved away the migraine attacks stopped instantly.

Hence, i saw the pain of the migraine was a spiritual sign for me to change that i was being attacked as i was living in the wrong place, amongst the wrong people for my soul, by making the changes i felt relieved and clear headed, spiritually more enlightened and with no more horrible migraine attacks!

# Directory of Sources of Spiritual Knowledge

## Our Spiritual Websites

www.heavensregister.com ספר קבלת שמים

An edition of this book "Heavens Register" for the internet.

## www.gilgulim.com

The Book of Reincarnation - Sefer Gilgulim by Reb Chaim Vital. Reb Chaim Vital, author of Sefer Gilgulim, the Book of Re-Incarnation, 1543 - 1620 (Yarzheit 2 Iyar 5380) Buried in Damascus - Syria , he lived in Israel Sefad and in Syria . A pupil of the Ari, he was respected worldwide both Ashkenazic and Sephardic Jews alike. Reb Chaim Vital was the author of many Kabbalist, Talmudic and Biblical works including Etz Chaim (Tree of Life) on Kabbala, and Lekutai Torah (Gleanings of Torah). He had sole possession of the Ari's writings, and most of our knowledge of the Ari's life and teachings are from Reb Chaim Vital. But without doubt the most famous and profound book he wrote was Sefer Gilgulim the Book of re-incarnation.

## www.eliyahuhanavi.org

The Famous Sefer - Book - Tana Devei Eliyahu ספר תנא דבי אליהו רבא וזוטא. The Tana Devei Eliyahu are the spiritual teachings of Eliyahu Hanavi and Rav Onan.

## MesillasYeshorim מסילת ישרים at
## www.famousrabbis.com/my/my.htm

All the classical spiritual works demonstrate that man must fear God. The Mesillas Yesharim tells us how.

## www.kavhayosher.com

Sefer Kav HaYosher ספר קב הישר, the book of Spiritual teachings by Reb Zvi Hirsch Kaindenover born Vilna; died at Frankfort-on-the-Main March 23, 1712, Yarzheit 15th Adar.

## www.sefershinuyim.com

The holy book Sefer Shinuyim - The Book of Changes ספר שינויים .
With deep spiritual insights to understand life in this physical world,
as a journey of transition, tests to correct and refine our souls.

## www.tikunim.com

The Principles of Sefer Tikunim - ספר תיקונים, are that we have created
an imperfect situation in our lives, through our actions, speech and
thoughts and disconnected ourselves from the Spirit world; this
website explains how to reconnect oneself.

## www.raziel.info

This is the website of true Jewish Astrology according to the Bible
Torah, true jewish astrology believes that GOD created the planets to
give our souls the energy to help us along our journey in this world.

Jewish spiritual astrology teaches that our journey in this life begins
40 days before conception (known as the SPIRITUAL birthday) and
the starts for real in this physical world on the day of conception.

## www.uziel.info

A website dedicated to the famous Rabbi Yonatan Ben Uziel - יונתן בן
עוזיאל, including prayer requests to his grave - tomb in Amuka Israel
especially for single people looking for one's soulmate.
www.uziel.info has a direct link to the Rabbi who says prayers daily,
at the Tomb of Yonatan Ben Uziel in Amuka, Israel for single people
in search of one's true soulmate.

## www.chidushim.com ספר חידושים

חידושי תורה של רוחניות - the website of spiritual torah teachings, the full
91 chapters of ספר חידושים Sefer Chidushim - Spiritual laws and
teachings, with inclusions of section שאלות ותשבות , questions and
answers regarding spiritual subjects and knowledge.

## www.22letters.com

This Website Shall Explain the Wonders, Mysteries, Meanings, Power, Strength and Pronunciation of Each of the "כב אותיות התורה" - The 22 Holy Letters of the Hebrew Alphabet.

Rabbi Akiva in his book אותיות רבי עקיבא explains the importance of the Hebrew language and the strength of power of praying in the original Hebrew language of 22 letters.

## www.yadpalmistry.com

חכמת יד "Chochmas Yad" The Book of "Wisdom of the knowledge of Palmistry".

Printed in the United Kingdom
by Lightning Source UK Ltd.
112311UKS00002B/223